Honest Questions

Honest Questions

A Personal Commentary
on Genesis 1 through 11

Edward B. Allen

Melbourne

Honest Questions: A Personal Commentary
on Genesis 1 through 11

by Edward B. Allen
Copyright © 2006, 2016 by Edward B. Allen
All rights reserved.
Reprinted with revisions, 2020, 2021, 2026.

Published by Edward B. Allen
Melbourne, Florida
Email: edward.allen1949@gmail.com

ISBN:
978-0-9974147-0-7 (paperback)
978-0-9974147-1-4 (ebook *.epub)
978-0-9974147-2-1 (Kindle ebook *.mobi)

Cover design by Ken Raney (http://kenraney.com).

To Angie, who loves me

Contents

Contents

Meditations

Preface

There are so many controversies over Genesis that I get confused. The many available books on Genesis, the Creation, and the Flood have not silenced all the noise. Why write yet another book about Genesis?

The same questions about Genesis chapters 1 through 11 keep coming out of these controversies over and over. I was unsatisfied both with traditional tidy answers and with evolutionists' arguments. So, I began to study Genesis, and this book is the result.

This book does not try to convince skeptics that God exists or that the Bible is true. Other books are about such debates. These issues are not controversial for me, because I have faith in God, and like most evangelicals, I believe that God inspired what is written in the Bible. This book is also not about whether mainstream science is valid, or whether Genesis agrees with scientific theories. Other books address these issues, and I don't have relevant expertise, even though I read what experts have to say.

I believe Genesis tells us about real people and historical events. My approach pays attention to the literary structure of the passages, rather than reading Genesis as if it were a newspaper with a literal writing style and full disclosure of facts. So, you may find my conclusions untraditional. This book investigates the controversial questions that are chapter titles, and then addresses other questions raised by each passage that have application to modern life. I identify with the people in the stories. The patriarchs are examples to me. Popular culture today is similar to ancient civilizations. I need God's perspective on modern culture. God is the same today as back then. I also share some devotional thoughts that deepened my worship. I hope that you will apply the Scriptures to your life as well.

Over the years, I have studied the Bible asking, "What does it say?" "What does it mean?" and "How does it apply to me?" These questions lead to learning about proper translation of Hebrew words, a sensible outline and interpretation, and application of scriptural principles. These three questions guide the organization of each chapter.

The *New American Standard Bible* (NASB) is the basis for the study. Other translations are also satisfactory. There are a few quotes from the *King James Version* (KJV), the *New King James Version* (NKJV), the *Holman Christian Standard Bible* (HCSB), and the *New International Version* (NIV). My outline is embedded in the quoted Scripture passages. I have made more paragraph breaks than the

NASB, because I follow the convention to begin a new paragraph when there is a new speaker in a dialogue or when the actor changes. I am not a scholar of the Hebrew language, but I carefully consider the opinions of those who are. I find literal translations of some words are helpful. So, my preferred translations of certain Hebrew words are shown **bold** when different from the NASB, and such translations are explained at the first occurrence with citations to sources. A word referred to as a word is in *italics*. Transliterated Hebrew words are also in *italics*, mostly in notes. I have adopted many word translations, cultural notes, and interpretations from a commentary by John Sailhamer (2008), who is an evangelical Bible scholar. I hope you will read his commentary for yourself. A major source for word translations is Strong's *Exhaustive Concordance of the Bible* (Strong, 1894) which includes a Hebrew dictionary. Strong's reference numbers for Hebrew words are used rather than full citations, for example, "(*Strong's* No. 776)." Some word translations are from text notes of the NIV (Barker, 1995).

Scripture references consist of book, chapter, verses, and version (if relevant), for example, "John 3:16 (KJV)." When Genesis is referenced, the book is omitted, for example, "1:3 (NASB)." All Scripture references are indexed. Clarifications of quotations are in [brackets]. Male pronouns are sometimes used to indicate a person of either gender. A citation is indicated by the name of the author and the year of publication, for example, "(Sailhamer, 2008)." Bibliographic details are in the References, so you can read my sources for yourself.

> Poetry is block-indented.
> Namings, blessings, and curses are also block-indented, even when they are not poetry.

I thank the American Scientific Affiliation (http://www.asa3.org) for their refereed academic journal, *Perspectives on Science and Christian Faith*, which has been an invaluable resource, as shown by the References. I thank Ron Chambers, Mike Constantine, Tony Hauck, and Gary Stebbins for their helpful comments. I also thank Jess Moore, Barbara Fraga, and Angela Krumins for their thoughtful comments on an early manuscript. Finally, I am thankful for the steadfast support of my wife, Angie.

E.B.A.

1

Introduction

Honest questions deserve honest answers.

Francis A. Schaeffer

Debates between Christians and atheists often focus on whether Genesis chapters 1 through 11 are true. A skeptic might say, "These stories are too weird to be true." "They are just myths." "Science has disproved Genesis." "God is unnecessary." "If Genesis isn't true then I won't believe the rest of the Bible." "How can you believe all that stuff?"

Naturally, many Christians feel they should defend the traditional stories. Because skeptics argue using science, some Christians try to show that the mainstream secular scientific theories are wrong, and thus, their opponents are wrong. Others try to harmonize Genesis with modern science. Other Christians say the stories are merely allegories, rather than history, so science is irrelevant. Most of us are just confused.

Each chapter title of this book poses a question that often comes out of such debates. We don't need to avoid honest questions. God is not embarrassed by our questions. He is the author of truth.[1] He wants our faith in Him to be founded on the truth.[2] I was unsatisfied both with traditional answers and with the arguments of atheists, so I launched my own study which became this book. Each chapter discusses the title question, gives personal insights into other deeper questions, and shares a devotional thought. I find that knowing God through his character and his actions is the real benefit of studying Genesis. For example, the narratives about the patriarchs tell us how God dealt with sin. Over and over, he imposed righteous judgment and extended mercy.

This book is not aimed to convince a skeptic to become a believer and will not help win points in a debate with an atheist. Faith in God and confidence in the Word of God, the Bible, is the starting point.

This book does not try to explain whether modern science and Genesis are compatible, nor does it argue whether secular mainstream science is valid.

---

[1] John 1:14.
[2] 2 Peter 1:16–21.

Even though it is fascinating to look at Genesis through the lens of modern science, I want to understand the early chapters as written and to grasp their message.

I believe that all of Scripture, including Genesis, is divinely inspired.[3] The Holy Spirit guided the author of Genesis as he selected and edited his material. He told us about the lives of real people and historical events. This study only covers Genesis 1 through 11. The remaining chapters in Genesis are not so controversial.

I sometimes take an untraditional approach to a passage. My interpretation is my opinion. I want to find interpretations that capture the meaning and impact of the passages. I know that you or your pastor might prefer a traditional interpretation. A difference in interpretation should never disrupt our fellowship in the Lord. Love for one another is more important than opinions.[4] I don't mind if you disagree with my opinions.

The remainder of this chapter presents my favorite outline and explains some general interpretative principles that I have used.

Outline

Any outline is the seed of an interpretation. Compare the outlines of commentators, and you will see why their interpretations differ. Formulating my outline below was the first step toward my interpretation of each passage. The first level of my outline is organized by the patriarchs: Adam, Noah, Shem, and Abraham. More about Abraham and stories about Isaac, Jacob, and Joseph come later in Genesis. The second level is based on literary relationships in the text. The third level reflects my interpretation of the passage.

I. ADAM

  A. CREATION OF THE SKY AND THE LAND

    1. Title   1:1

    2. First Day

       Day *vs.* Night   1:2–5

    3. Second Day

       Waters *vs.* Clouds   1:6–8

    4. Third Day

       Land *vs.* Seas   1:9–10

       Vegetables *vs.* Fruit   1:11–13

---

[3] 2 Timothy 3:16–17.
[4] 1 Corinthians 13:2.

C. PROMISE   12:1-4, ff.

(The story of Abraham continues.)

Frequently in Genesis, the end of a section is marked by poetry followed by a narrative epilogue (Sailhamer, 2008, pp. 34–35). The ends of some sections are marked by namings, blessings, or curses followed by a narrative epilogue, even though the naming, blessing, or curse is not poetry, *per se*. For example, 4:25–26 names Seth and Enosh followed by a remark. Also frequently in Hebrew narrative writing, the same literary feature will appear at the beginning and at the end of a section, framing the section. For example, 4:15 and 4:24 both talk about vengeance, framing the section. The outline above follows such markers and frames. Details are discussed below with each passage.

This study covers the narratives about the patriarchs Adam, Noah, and Shem, and begins the story of Abraham. The story of Adam (1:1–6:4) is introduced by the Creation. The "Fall" is the traditional title for the story of Adam's and Eve's sin. The story of Adam's sons, Cain and Abel, is also included in the story of Adam. The story of Adam is framed by the Genealogy of the Sky and the Land (2:4–24) near the beginning and the Genealogy of Mankind (5:1–6:4) at the end. Noah is introduced near the end of this genealogy.[5]

The story of Noah (6:5–9:29) is introduced by describing the Corruption of the Land (6:5–8) and includes the story of the Flood. The story of Noah is framed by the Genealogy of Noah (6:9–10) near the beginning and the completion of the Genealogy of Mankind at the end (9:28–29).

The story of Shem tells us little about him personally. It includes the story of the Tower of Babel. The story of Shem begins with the Genealogy of Shem, Ham, and Japheth (10:1–32) and ends with the Genealogy of Shem (11:10–26). Abraham (Abram) is introduced at the end of this genealogy.[6]

The story of Abraham begins with the Genealogy of Terah (11:27–31) and the completion of the Genealogy of Shem (11:32). The stories about Abraham and the other patriarchs continue in the later chapters of Genesis, which are beyond the scope of this book.

Interpreting Genesis

According to tradition, Moses was the author of Genesis (Sailhamer, 2008, p. 25) and he lived about 1500–1400 BC. Egypt, Mesopotamia, and nearby regions had thriving civilizations. Written records were commonly used for government and business. Trade actively spanned from Greece to India. I like to ask, "What would Moses think about that?" I want to keep Moses and his times in mind, and interpret Genesis in a way that would make sense to the original audience.

---

[5] 5:28–32.
[6] 11:26.

The Hebrew language and references to ancient life have considerable uncertainty and ambiguity. Some passages are just too vague to satisfy the curious. Controversies over Genesis often ask questions that are impossible to answer. Even though I know the opinions of experts, I prefer to accept the ambiguity, and avoid wrong conclusions by saying "I don't know."

For example, where did Moses get his information? Moses was obviously not an eye-witness to the events described in Genesis. Archeologists have found that written records were common even before the time of Abraham, so written stories could have been passed down through the family for many generations. The Bible does not say whether Moses had written records. The Bible also does not say that the stories of Genesis were dictated by God on Mount Sinai. This is an example of a question that is impossible to answer. I don't know where Moses got his information, and it doesn't really matter.

Scientific data should agree with the Scriptures whenever they address the same event. The Bible is true, because it is inspired by God. Scientific data is true, because it is the evidence of what God has done. What God says and what he has done are compatible. So a sound interpretation must determine when modern scientific data and the Scriptures address the same event. In this book, I minimize analysis of scientific data and theories, because others have done so extensively. Whether science is compatible with Genesis has been an area of controversy both between Christians and skeptics and among Christians who work in science. This issue is outside the scope of this book.

Many approach Genesis as if it is a daily newspaper, expecting it to conform to modern standards of journalism, such as chronological narratives, complete disclosure of facts, a scientific understanding of nature, and a literal (non-figurative) writing style. The Bible has many genres of literature, but a modern newspaper is not one of them. This newspaper mentality interprets the Scriptures with a modern world-view that was unknown in ancient times. Genesis is not a newspaper. God was not a celestial newspaper reporter, but he did inspire godly men like Moses to write the Scriptures.[7]

For example, Cain's wife is mentioned,[8] but the passage does not talk about the birth of any girls. Where did she come from? This is an awkward fact when reading Genesis like a newspaper. Genesis tells us about the origin of Adam and Eve, and then we read about the births of Cain and Abel. Nowhere do we read about the birth of Cain's wife. Unlike a newspaper, the passage does not disclose all the facts. Who was Cain's wife? Apparently such details were not important.

Everyone who interprets Genesis faces the challenge of discerning the factual from the poetic. That is one reason Christians disagree sometimes. I make it clear when I think a passage was intended to be poetic and why.

For example, God said to Cain that Abel's blood cried out and that the ground opened its mouth.[9] Everyone knows that blood does not have vocal

---

[7]Hebrews 1:1 and 2 Timothy 3:16–17.

[8]4:17.

[9]4:10–11.

chords and the ground does not have a mouth. These phrases are clearly a figurative description of God's knowledge of Abel's murder.

It is vital to interpret a Scripture so that it is meaningful across all cultures and eras of God's people. God's Word is for all people, so an interpretation should be general enough to be relevant to all. That is why I avoid an interpretation that is dependent on modern scientific knowledge. In contrast, an application of a Scripture is often very personal, narrow, and specific to today. So it is important to distinguish interpretation from application.

For example, the story of Cain and Abel ends with the birth of Seth.[10] Through his birth, God comforted grieving Eve whose son had been murdered by his brother. I can apply this event whenever I am grieving over a tragic loss. God will give me comfort and a way for restoration like he did for Eve.

In summary, my aim is a sound interpretation. I will consider the culture and times of the original audience. I will recognize when the Hebrew text is vague or ambiguous. I will set aside questions that the text does not address. I will consider modern science to be relevant only when it speaks to the same events as the text. I will interpret according to the genre of the text. I won't read Genesis like a newspaper. I will discern when the Hebrew text is poetry or speaks figuratively. A sound interpretation will be general enough to be understood by God's people in all eras and cultures, and will be helpful in application to my local times and situation.

---

[10] 4:25.

Part I

Adam

2

How long did Creation take?

> In the beginning God created the heaven and the earth.
>
> Genesis 1:1 (KJV)

Astronomers have found evidence of a Big Bang (Johnson, 1994; Phillips, 2005). They agree with Genesis 1:1—the universe had a beginning. They consider the beginning of the universe to be when all matter and energy exploded from a single point. In verse 1, *beginning*[1] means the starting point of a specific duration. This corresponds to an end.[2] Sailhamer (2008, p. 51) points out that the first Hebrew word of the Bible implies that the world had a beginning and will have an end. The first chapter of the Bible explains the beginning. The last chapters of the Bible explain the end.[3] Peter gives us a picture of what the end will be like.

> But the day of the Lord will come like a thief, in which the heavens will pass away with a roar and the elements will be destroyed with intense heat, and the earth and its works will be burned up.
>
> 2 Peter 3:10 (NASB)

Let us take a close look at what the Scripture says about Creation. In this chapter, we focus on the first three days.

Genesis 1:1–13 (NASB)

I. ADAM

A. CREATION OF THE SKY AND THE LAND

1. Title

---

[1] The Hebrew word *re'sit* (*Strong's* No. 7225).
[2] The Hebrew word *'aharit* (*Strong's* No. 319).
[3] Revelation 21:1–22:5.

CHAPTER 1

1 In the beginning God created the **sky** and the **land**.

2. First Day

Day *vs.* Night

2 The **land** was formless and void, and darkness was over the surface of the deep, and the Spirit of God was moving over the surface of the waters. 3 **And** God said, "Let there be light"; and there was light. 4 God saw that the light was good; and God separated the light from the darkness. 5 God called the light day, and the darkness He called night. And there was evening and there was morning, one day.

3. Second Day

Waters *vs.* Clouds

6 **And** God said, "Let there be an expanse in the midst of the waters, and let it separate the waters from the waters." 7 God made the expanse, and separated the waters which were below the expanse from the waters which were above the expanse; and it was so. 8 God called the expanse **sky**. And there was evening and there was morning, a second day.

4. Third Day

Land *vs.* Seas

9 **And** God said, "Let the waters below the **sky** be gathered into one place, and let the dry land appear"; and it was so. 10 God called the dry **ground land**, and the gathering of the waters He called seas; and God saw that it was good.

Vegetables *vs.* Fruit

11 **And** God said, "Let the **land** sprout vegetation, plants yielding seed, and fruit trees on the **land** bearing fruit after their kind with seed in them"; and it was so. 12 The **land** brought forth vegetation, plants yielding seed after their kind, and trees bearing fruit with seed in them, after their kind; and God saw that it was good. 13 There was evening and there was morning, a third day.

The outline of the Creation story[4] is clear from the text. The end of each of the first six days of Creation is marked by the same phrase, "There was evening, and there was morning, a [such and such] day."

The Hebrew word translated *heavens*[5] in verse 1 is literally translated **sky**

---

[4]1:1–2:3.
[5]The Hebrew word *samayim* (*Strong's* No. 8064).

and the Hebrew word translated *earth*[6] means **land**. Most English translations, like the NASB, use *heavens* and *earth*, implying the cosmos and Planet Earth, which are modern concepts, unknown to the ancient world (Tanner, 1997). Translating these words to imply the cosmos and Planet Earth misrepresents the literal sense of the passage. In this book, I consistently translate these as **sky** and **land** in boldface type, when different from the NASB, to emphasize that the cosmos and the Planet Earth were not literally intended. We look up and we see the **sky**. We look down and we see dirt—the **land**.

Like the traditional interpretation, I interpret the text of verse 1, "**sky** and **land**," as everything. From a modern perspective, we apply this to mean the entire universe, including Planet Earth. It is important to distinguish the literal translation from an interpretation and from an application.

The NASB uses the word *then* in each of the days of Creation. I consistently translate this conjunction in the Hebrew text as **and** which is its usual translation. The NASB is in effect interpreting the passage as chronological order.

How long did Creation take?

In 2013, observations from the Planck spacecraft, sponsored by the European Space Agency, were used to refine the estimated time since the Big Bang (Jet Propulsion Laboratory, 2013)—about 13.8 billion years—which astronomers consider to be the age of the universe. Astronomers were very excited to get more precise data than ever before. From that starting point, astronomers think the universe slowly became what we see today. However, the traditional interpretation of Genesis 1 asserts that the Creation happened in seven 24-hour days for a total of only one week. This mismatch is confusing.

How long did Creation take? This question is the first one that skeptics want to argue about. They say it is obvious that the Bible is wrong.

Some Christians argue that Planet Earth is much younger than the several billion years estimated by modern science. Other Christians offer scenarios and interpretations to show that Genesis 1 is compatible with an old Planet Earth. I will let others sort through the proposed interpretations to figure out which is most compatible with science. Let us focus on gaining a sound understanding of the passage.

Many details of the Creation story are not explained for a scientific audience. For example, the cause of the darkness in 1:2 is not explained, nor is the origin of the formless land. Even though I may be curious about the scientific background, these details apparently were not important to the author. Genesis 1 describes the Creation from a human viewpoint, rather than a scientific one. I can imagine the author looking around at all that God has made. As he wrote this passage, he used ordinary words to describe what he could see, rather than scientific details. The Creation story is not a science lesson.

The passage frequently says "God said ... and it was so" (NASB),[7] but does

---

[6]The Hebrew word *'eres* (*Strong's* No. 776).
[7]1:3, 6–7, 9, 11, 14–15, 24, 29–30.

not say what happened between the moment he spoke and the moment it was so. The traditional interpretation assumes that "it was so" happened instantly after "God said." This is due to reading the passage like a newspaper, where modern journalism standards call for complete chronological narratives. Because the passage does not describe anything between "God said" and "it was so," many assume nothing happened. However, the process of creation is not explained. Maybe a lot of things happened, but the author did not say. The Creation story is not a newspaper report.

Evening and *morning* (NASB) are traditionally interpreted as only one sunset and one sunrise, hinting at one 24-hour day. How long is a day from God's perspective?

> But do not let this one fact escape your notice, beloved, that with the Lord one day is like a thousand years, and a thousand years like one day.
>
> 2 Peter 3:8 (NASB)

The eternal God is not limited by our sense of time. This verse opens the door to interpreting *day* here as a long period of time, just like in 2:4 (NASB) and 2:17 (NASB). Similar figurative usage is in many other places in the Bible. The passage does not say that a day was 24 hours (Kline, 1996).

In summary, the author of Genesis does not use scientific jargon. He uses ordinary words like *land* and *sky*, rather than *Planet Earth* and the *universe*. The starting point of a dark formless land[8] is not explained. The process of creation is not explained. The Creation story is not a science lesson. The story does not disclose what happened between "God said" and "it was so." The Creation story is not a newspaper story with complete chronological facts. The word *day* is ambiguous and I think it is figurative in this passage. God's perspective on time is not the same as ours.

The traditional answer to "How long did Creation take?" is six twenty-four hour days. I conclude that Genesis does not tell us how long Creation took, because the word *day* can be interpreted as an indefinite era.

Who created the universe?

Scientific data is silent regarding who was responsible for Creation. Atheists then conclude that the Creator does not exist.[9] They say that only impersonal processes formed our world with all its manifold wonders. Atheists pretend that the Creator is not there, but the evidence is right before their eyes.

> For since the creation of the world His invisible attributes, His eternal power and divine nature, have been clearly seen, being understood through what has been made, so that they are without excuse.
>
> Romans 1:20 (NASB)

---

[8]1:2.
[9]Psalms 14:1.

Rather than the "How long?" question, the passage answers the "Who?" question. Who created the universe? The answer is God did. The names of God in Genesis were carefully chosen to add literary impact to the message of each section.[10] In verse 1, *God*[11] is the Creator's title. This title is systematically used in this section. This fits the passage, which is the Creation story.

The New Testament explains that Jesus Christ, God's Son, was there from the beginning. He was the agent who made all things, both physical and spiritual.[12]

> For by Him all things were created, both in the heavens and on earth, visible and invisible, whether thrones or dominions or rulers or authorities—all things have been created through Him and for Him.
>
> Colossians 1:16 (NASB)

When I look around at creation, the way the author of Genesis did, I see that God's power and wisdom are far beyond mine. I am focused on knowing the Creator of the universe and his love for me. He loves skeptics, too, and wants a relationship with each person. "Who created the universe?" is the important question to me. The Creation story says who made our world. God personally created it.

---

[10]For example, 2:4, 4:1, and 5:1.
[11]The Hebrew word *'elohim* (*Strong's* No. 430).
[12]John 1:1–3.

Who made the night?

Read Genesis 1:4–5.

If I say, "Surely the darkness will overwhelm me,
And the light around me will be night,"
Even the darkness is not dark to You,
And the night is as bright as the day.
Darkness and light are alike to You.

Psalms 139:11–12 (NASB)

We had a large tree that dropped its figs in the backyard. In the daylight, I could see I had a cleanup job ahead of me. In the middle of the night, the floodlight came on automatically. Living in the suburbs, we were surprised to see a fox and some raccoons cleaning up the figs. This happened night after night for a couple of weeks. God provided night for that fox and those raccoons to get their dinner at our house.

To human eyes, the night hides, but darkness is not dark to the creator of day and night. Life's situations may be confusing, and I cannot see one step in front of the next in the darkness. But the Lord sees everything and he holds my hand. He sees me when sleeping, and he sees the fox when dining, because he made the night.

PRAYER: Lord, even though I may not see the way ahead in life, I know that you are faithful and in my darkness, you see the path I should take. Amen.

3

Did evolution really happen?

O Lord, how many are Your works!
In wisdom You have made them all;
The earth is full of Your possessions.
There is the sea, great and broad,
In which are swarms without number,
Animals both small and great.

Psalms 104:24–25 (NASB)

When I took Biology class, I was astounded at the intricacies of living things. The more I learn about God's creation, the more amazed I become. Each of God's creatures has its own special abilities. The number of distinct species is overwhelming. Ecological systems are so complex that biologists can only sketch the outlines.

The previous chapter discussed the first three days of Creation. This chapter focuses on the remaining four days when the animals were created.

Genesis 1:14–2:3 (NASB)

---

5. Fourth Day

Days *vs.* Seasons *vs.* Years

14 **And** God said, "Let there be lights in the expanse of the **sky** to separate the day from the night, and let them be for signs and for seasons and for days and years; 15 and let them be for lights in the expanse of the **sky** to give light on the **land**"; and it was so. 16 God made the two great lights, the greater light to govern the day, and the lesser light to govern the night; He made the stars also. 17 God placed them in the expanse of the **sky** to give light on the **land**, 18 and to govern the day and the night, and to separate the light

from the darkness; and God saw that it was good. 19 There was evening and there was morning, a fourth day.

> 6. Fifth Day

Sea Animals *vs.* Birds

20 **And** God said, "Let the waters teem with swarms of living creatures, and let birds fly above the **land** in the open expanse of the **sky**." 21 God created the great sea monsters and every living creature that moves, with which the waters swarmed after their kind, and every winged bird after its kind; and God saw that it was good. 22 God blessed them, saying,

> "Be fruitful and multiply,
> and fill the waters in the seas,
> and let birds multiply on the **land**."

23 There was evening and there was morning, a fifth day.

> 7. Sixth Day

Livestock *vs.* Creepers *vs.* Wild Animals

24 **And** God said, "Let the **land** bring forth living creatures after their kind: cattle and creeping things and beasts of the **land** after their kind"; and it was so. 25 God made the beasts of the **land** after their kind, and the cattle after their kind, and everything that creeps on the ground after its kind; and God saw that it was good.

Mankind: Male *vs.* Female

26 **And** God said, "Let Us make **mankind** in Our image, according to Our likeness; and let them rule over the fish of the sea and over the birds of the sky and over the cattle and over all the **land**, and over every creeping thing that creeps on the **land**." 27 God created **mankind** in His own image, in the image of God He created him; male and female He created them. 28 God blessed them; and God said to them,

> "Be fruitful and multiply,
> and fill the **land**,
> and subdue it;
> and rule over the fish of the sea
> and over the birds of the sky
> and over every living thing that moves on the **land**."

29 **And** God said, "Behold, I have given you every plant yielding seed that is on the surface of all the **land**, and every tree which has fruit yielding seed; it shall be food for you; 30 and to every beast of the **land** and to every bird of the sky and to every thing that moves on the **land** which has life, I have given every green plant for food"; and it was so. 31 God saw all that He had made, and behold, it was

very good. And there was evening and there was morning, the sixth day.

8. Seventh Day

Work *vs.* Rest

CHAPTER 2

1 Thus the **sky** and the **land** were completed, and all their hosts.
2 By the seventh day God completed His work which He had done, and He rested on the seventh day from all His work which He had done.

3 **And** God blessed the seventh day and sanctified it, because in it He rested from all His work which God had created and made.

As discussed in the previous chapter, the outline is structured according to the days of Creation. Rather than ending with the phrase, "There was evening, and there was morning ...," the seventh day ends with a blessing followed by a short narrative epilogue,[1] marking the end of the Creation section. The number of days of Creation, seven, indicates that Creation was complete. Throughout the Scriptures, seven is associated with completeness or wholeness. Evening and morning are not mentioned on the seventh day, because it is the end of this section.

The Hebrew word translated *man*[2] has several translations in Genesis. In this study, I consistently translate this Hebrew word as (1) **mankind**, if both male and female are indicated by the context, such as in 1:27 and 5:1, (2) **the man**, if preceded by the definite article (*the*), such as in 3:20, and (3) the proper name **Adam**, if an individual is clearly indicated by the context and it is not preceded by the definite article, such as in 5:3. These are **bold**, if different from the NASB.

Did evolution really happen?

Schools across America have seen bitter battles over teaching evolution. Atheists want to exclude any discussion of Genesis. They say religion does not belong in the science classroom. The Christians want the traditional Creation story presented to children. There does not seem to be a middle ground.

Science proposes theories to explain data from fossils and genetics. The theory of evolution does not address the origin of life, but it does try to explain the variety of life. The modern theory of evolution claims that a huge number of random events changed the DNA of organisms over a very long time, resulting in the development of all the various forms of life.

---

[1] 2:3.
[2] The Hebrew word *'adam* (*Strong's* No. 120).

Because science considers only natural data, it is silent about God's role. However, the theory of evolution does not exclude God, because he is Lord of random events.

> The lot is cast into the lap,
> But its every decision is from the Lord.
>
> Proverbs 16:33 (NASB)

What God did with purpose might appear to be random to a scientist who is limited to data from fossils and genetics. Did evolution really happen?

I can hear someone protest, "But God wouldn't side with atheists!" God does not care about which side atheists are on. He just goes about his own business.

How did God create all the variety of life? In this section, we focus on all life, not primarily the origin of mankind. Of course, if Creation took only seven twenty-four hour days, evolution would be impossible. Assuming an old Planet Earth, let us consider other issues regarding the creation of the variety of life.

If evolution really happened, then the order of events in Scripture should match the chronological order of fossil data. Fossils are buried in layers of rock. Older fossils are found in the lower layers, so the order is pretty clear.

The Creation story is organized into seven days. The traditional interpretation assumes that *one day, second, third,* and so on mean chronological order. Let's compare the order of days in Genesis 1 to the order of events in scientific data.

The traditional interpretation of Genesis 1 places the creation of the land and seas on the third day and places the creation of the sun, moon, and stars later on the fourth day.[3] Astronomers and geologists think that the order of appearance at the beginning of the universe was (1) stars, (2) our sun, (3) Planet Earth, (4) the moon, (5) seas, and (6) land. So, the order of the traditional interpretation is different from that of science. Considering the nuances of Hebrew grammar, Sailhamer (2008, pp. 64–65) translates the beginning of verse 14 as "And God said, 'Let the lights in the expanse of the sky separate ...' " This implies that the sun, moon, and stars already existed. In contrast, most English translations say, "Let there be lights ..." Thus in Sailhamer's view, the supposed conflict with astronomy disappears, because the sun, moon, and stars were created some time before the fourth day.

According to the traditional interpretation, fish and birds were created on the fifth day, and land animals and mankind were created afterwards on the sixth day. However, fossils indicate that many land animals were on Planet Earth before birds appeared. For example, most dinosaurs lived before any birds existed. Does the order of fossils contradict Genesis 1?

The Creation story has an elaborate literary structure that yields insights about the order of Creation. The following presents three aspects of this structure.

---

[3]1:16.

The six days of Creation have a symmetric literary structure (Barker, 1995, s.v. 1:11) (Sailhamer, 2008, p. 52). Each of the first three days corresponds to one of the latter three days, as shown in the following list.

- Day 1 and day 4: Light corresponds to lights in the sky.

- Day 2 and day 5: Waters and sky correspond to sea creatures and birds.

- Day 3 and day 6: Land corresponds to land animals and mankind.

Apparently, the author delayed discussing the lights until the fourth day so that the story could have this symmetry. The sea creatures and birds are paired so there could be symmetry with seas and clouds which are both water.

A second literary analysis shows that the Creation story is about preparing the land for mankind (Sailhamer, 2008, pp. 54–55). The seven days of Creation describe what the Creator did for the benefit of mankind from a human point of view. The living God took the initiative to create a place for mankind. Sailhamer (2008, p. 57) emphasizes that God knows what is good for mankind. Every created thing is not itemized, because the focus is on things relevant to mankind. The following list shows how the creation benefits mankind.

- Days 1 and 2: Light and water are necessary for agriculture.

- Days 3 and 4: Food grows on the land during seasons.

- Days 5 and 6: Animals and mankind live in the environment.

- Day 7: Mankind and domestic animals need rest.

For example, on the first day,[4] the land was uninhabitable, so God prepared it for mankind. On the third day,[5] the land was good because it was now inhabitable.

On the third day, only bushes and trees that are good for mankind's food[6] are mentioned. Other plants are not interesting.

On the fourth day,[7] *to separate* (NASB) emphasizes that God assigned a purpose to the sun, moon, and stars, namely, to distinguish day from night. He also assigned them the purpose of marking the seasons for the benefit of mankind.

Verse 24 speaks generally about wild animals on the sixth day, but does not specifically say that God made the dinosaurs. Fossils indicate that all dinosaurs lived millions of years before the earliest humans. Thus, dinosaurs are not relevant to things that benefit mankind.

Our outline has a third literary structure. As shown below, each day of creation involved separation, that is, making distinctions.

---

[4] 1:2.
[5] 1:10.
[6] 1:11, 29.
[7] 1:14.

- Day 1: Day *vs.* Night (1:3)

- Day 2: Waters *vs.* Clouds (1:7)

- Day 3: Land *vs.* Seas (1:9)

- Day 3: Vegetables *vs.* Fruit (1:11)

- Day 4: Days *vs.* Seasons *vs.* Years (1:14)

- Day 5: Sea Animals *vs.* Birds (1:20)

- Day 6: Livestock *vs.* Creepers *vs.* Wild Animals (1:24)

- Day 6: Mankind: Male *vs.* Female (1:27)

- Day 7: Work *vs.* Rest (2:3)

For example, on the sixth day,[8] two kinds of humans are distinguished, male and female. The gender of animals was not of interest, even though most animals are male and female, too.

These three kinds of literary symmetry indicate that the order of the days was carefully crafted to cover all the topics (Kline, 1996). Coverage of the topics was more important than the chronological sequence of events. Thus, it is misleading to interpret the passage like a chronological newspaper story. The seven days of Creation are like a tapestry where we see the whole at one time. So, I think the ordinal numbers (one day, second, third, etc.) are the order of presentation, not the chronological order of events. Genesis 1 does not try to explain the order that various forms of life were created. The chronological order observed in fossils does not contradict the message of the Creation story, because Genesis 1 does not present the chronological order.

It is my opinion that the Bible does not tell us whether modern scientific theories are correct, and the Bible does not deny that evolution happened.

Why did God create life?

Rather than answer how God created the variety of life, Genesis 1 answers the "Why?" question. Why did God create life?

There were three blessings of Creation. The first blessing of Creation was the gift of procreation. Offspring are gifts from the Creator to the creatures of the sea, the sky,[9] and the land. From our modern vantage point, "all their hosts" in 2:1 reminds us of the enormous number of living things that fill Planet Earth.

The second blessing of Creation was the gift of dominion.[10] The gift of dominion is the scriptural basis for mankind's responsibility to take good care

---

[8]1:27.
[9]1:20–22.
[10]1:28.

of the natural environment. Perhaps the parade of environmental disasters that we see in the news today means selfish mankind has not done a very good job in stewardship of the environment.

The third blessing of Creation was rest.[11] The seventh day was set apart from the others (Sabbath). God wants all of his creatures, and people in particular, to have rest.

Genesis 1 answers the "Why?" question. God made the world to provide a good place for mankind to live. God blessed mankind in three ways. These three blessings remind us of the many other ways that God has blessed us as well.

God's purpose in creating the world is apparent in the little things of life. The Creator of the universe is the same God who is concerned about every aspect of my life.[12] He has made a good place for me, both in this life[13] and in eternity.[14] My thankful heart responds with worship. Why God created the world is more important to me than knowing whether evolution really happened, because knowing why gives me a deeper appreciation for the Creator.

---

[11] 2:3.
[12] Psalms 139:1–6.
[13] 2 Peter 1:3.
[14] John 14:1–3.

Dominion

Read Genesis 1:26–28.

The Lord God took the man and placed him in the garden of Eden to work it and watch over it.

Genesis 2:15 (HCSB)

I've been planting shrubs in the backyard. I'm expecting the flowers to provide bees and butterflies with the nectar they crave. The mockingbirds and the squirrels will feast on the berries. God gave me this backyard to manage, so I want to give back to God's birds, insects, and wild animals that are my neighbors. The Creator has blessed me with the gift of dominion, so I must use it wisely. He wants this backyard to be well tended.

I am the Lord's gardener. He wants me to love him, love others, care for the weak, and keep a pure heart. Like tending my backyard, I must wisely perform the responsibilities in life he has given me.

PRAYER: Lord, thank you for the gift of dominion in my backyard. Give me your love for those around me. Give me your wisdom to do what you want me to do. By the way, I need your help in the backyard, too. Amen.

4

Did mankind come from monkeys?

For You formed my inward parts;
You wove me in my mother's womb.

Psalms 139:13 (NASB)

In 1859, Charles Darwin published his seminal book, *On the Origin of Species*. His theory of evolution seemed to say that mankind was descended from monkeys. In that era, one's ancestry was the basis for self-respect and one's place in society. The queen held her position because of royal ancestry. The aristocracy inherited their titles from their fathers. Having a respected family was important. Everyone knew that being God's special creation made us better than monkeys. I imagine that the idea of being a descendant of a monkey was pretty insulting. In modern times, his theory has been elaborated and is widely assumed to be irrefutable truth, making God unnecessary.

The previous chapter studied the creation on the sixth day, and the variety of all life. In this chapter, let us consider the origin of mankind.

Genesis 2:4–24 (NASB)

B. GENEALOGY OF THE SKY AND THE LAND

1. Title

4 This is the **genealogy** of the **sky** and the **land** when they were created, in the day that the Lord God made **land** and **sky**.

2. Gift of Life

5 Now no shrub of the field was yet in the **land**, and no plant of the field had yet sprouted, for the Lord God had not sent rain upon the **land**, and there was no **mankind** to cultivate the ground.

6 But a mist used to rise from the **land** and water the whole surface of the ground. 7 Then the Lord God formed **mankind** of dust from the ground, and breathed into his nostrils the breath of life; and **mankind** became a living being.

3. Gift of Food

8 The Lord God planted a garden toward the east, in Eden; and there He placed the man whom He had formed. 9 Out of the ground the Lord God caused to grow every tree that is pleasing to the sight and good for food; the tree of life also in the midst of the garden, and the tree of the knowledge of good and evil.

10 Now a river flowed out of Eden to water the garden; and from there it divided and became four rivers. 11 The name of the first is Pishon; it flows around the whole land of Havilah, where there is gold. 12 The gold of that land is good; the bdellium and the onyx stone are there. 13 The name of the second river is Gihon; it flows around the whole land of Cush. 14 The name of the third river is Tigris; it flows east of Assyria. And the fourth river is the Euphrates.

15 Then the Lord God took the man and put him into the garden of Eden to cultivate it and keep it. 16 The Lord God commanded the man, saying, "From any tree of the garden you may eat freely; 17 but from the tree of the knowledge of good and evil you shall not eat, for in the day that you eat from it you will surely die."

4. Gift of a Helper

18 Then the Lord God said, "It is not good for the man to be alone; I will make him a helper suitable for him." 19 Out of the ground the Lord God formed every beast of the field and every bird of the sky, and brought them to the man to see what he would call them; and whatever the man called a living creature, that was its name. 20 The man gave names to all the cattle, and to the birds of the sky, and to every beast of the field, but for **mankind** there was not found a helper suitable for him. 21 So the Lord God caused a deep sleep to fall upon the man, and he slept; then He took one of his ribs and closed up the flesh at that place. 22 The Lord God fashioned into a **wife** the rib which He had taken from the man, and brought her to the man.

23 The man said,

"This is now bone of my bones,
And flesh of my flesh;
She shall be called **wife**,
Because she was taken out of **husband**."

24 For this reason a **husband** shall leave his father and his mother, and be joined to his wife; and they shall become one flesh.

The word *account* (NASB)[1] has a broad definition. In Genesis, it denotes a section of the story. Even though an account sometimes contains narrative, I consistently translate it **genealogy**, because such passages often consist of lists of fathers and sons. Chapter 2 largely consists of the Genealogy of the Sky and the Land.[2] The end of the section is marked by poetry[3] and a narrative epilogue.[4] Many commentators (Sailhamer, 2008, p. 74) consider this section to be an elaboration of what happened on the sixth day of Creation, because both passages talk about the creation of mankind and the animals.

The Creation story in chapter 1 systematically uses the Creator's title, *God*. In this section, *Lord God* (NASB)[5] is systematically used. *Lord* refers to his personal name; *God* is his title as Creator. This fits the passage, because his goal in Creation was personal fellowship with mankind.

The previous chapter explains my literal translations of **man**.[6] The word *woman* (NASB)[7] has multiple translations. The basic meaning is woman; another meaning is wife. In this study, I consistently translate it as **wife**. In 2:23, *woman* and *man* (NASB) is wordplay in Hebrew. Here, the word *man* (NASB),[8] which also means husband, is a different Hebrew word from the above word for *man*.[9] I translate this word in 2:23 as **husband** to correspond to **wife**, and to distinguish it from **man**.

Did mankind come from monkeys?

In 1925, John Scopes, a high school biology teacher in the small town of Dayton, Tennessee, was charged with illegally teaching the theory of evolution (Linder, 2000).[10] The trial was a sensational news event. High-profile legal teams from across the nation were assembled for the prosecution and the defense. William Jennings Bryan[11] was the principal spokesman for the prosecution, and Clarence Darrow for the defense. The press, which was largely sympathetic to evolution, portrayed the trial as a showdown of traditional values and beliefs versus modern values and beliefs. The trial became known as

---

[1]2:4. The Hebrew word *toledot* (*Strong's* No. 8435). English translations use a variety of English words for this Hebrew word, such as *account* (2:4 (NASB) and NIV), *generations* (KJV and 5:1 (NASB)), *genealogy* (5:1 (NKJV)), *history* (2:4 (NKJV)), and others.

[2]2:4–24.

[3]2:23.

[4]2:24.

[5]The Hebrew word *yhwh* (*Strong's* No. 3068). The Hebrew word *'elohim* (*Strong's* No. 430). Since ancient times, Jews have been reluctant to pronounce God's personal name *yhwh*, because it is holy, so it became customary to say the Hebrew word for *Lord* instead. Many modern translations, such as the NASB, follow this custom.

[6]The Hebrew word *'adam* (*Strong's* No. 120).

[7]2:22–23. The Hebrew word *'ishah* (*Strong's* No. 802).

[8]The Hebrew word *'ish* (*Strong's* No. 376).

[9]The Hebrew word *'adam* (*Strong's* No. 120).

[10]The purpose of the case was to test the legality of the Tennessee law.

[11]William Jennings Bryan is best known for his career as a politician. He was a candidate for President of the United States in 1896.

the Scopes Monkey Trial.[12]

The issues publicized by this trial have continued to reverberate in American culture. Evolutionism has become entrenched in the education system. Many have abandoned faith in the Creator in favor of faith in an impersonal evolutionary process. Are traditional beliefs wrong? Are modern values better? Did mankind come from monkeys?

The modern scientific theory of evolution claims that mankind and monkeys came from a common ancestor. Each time a human-like or monkey-like fossil is discovered, scientists speculate whether it is the "missing link." They talk on and on about homonids, neanderthals, homo sapiens, and anatomically modern man. The origin of mankind is a favorite topic of atheists when trying to discredit the Bible.

The passage uses the word *formed* (NASB)[13] to evoke the familiar image of a potter to describe what the Lord God did when he made mankind. A traditional literal interpretation assumes this is a realistic image, like a newspaper photograph. However, Genesis is not a newspaper report. I think making a doctrine based on one word, *formed*, is not warranted. Because the Lord God is spirit, I interpret the image of a potter figuratively. The passage does not explain the details of the process, nor does it say how long the process took. The phrase "formed **mankind** of dust"[14] emphasizes the material that a human body is made of, and points to mankind's mortality.[15] The passage specifies the result, mankind's body is the same stuff as the soil.

The passage does not say whether anatomically modern mankind's body was descended from a common ancestor with monkeys. I do know that the origin of mankind was in the heart of the Lord God, and it was not an accident.

What is mankind's purpose?

Rather than answer the origins process question, Genesis answers the question, "What is mankind's purpose?"

The Lord God placed one man in the Garden of Eden and gave him a job to do. Sailhamer (2008, pp. 79–80) argues that the genders of the Hebrew verbs indicate that the phrase *cultivate it and keep it* (NASB)[16] should be translated as *worship and obey*.

The Lord God equipped mankind to fulfill his purpose. As shown in our outline, this passage describes three gifts that the Lord God gave to mankind: the gift of life, the gift of food, and the gift of a helper. James explains that good gifts come from the Lord.

---

[12] As expected, Mr. Scopes was found guilty, and was fined $100. Upon appeal, the conviction was overturned on a technicality, and the case was dropped.

[13] The Hebrew word *yatsar* (*Strong's* No. 3335).

[14] 2:7.

[15] See also 3:19.

[16] 2:15.

> Every good thing given and every perfect gift is from above, coming down from the Father of lights, with whom there is no variation or shifting shadow.
>
> James 1:17 (NASB)

The gift of life. The first gift to mankind was life itself.[17] Genesis 2 clearly teaches that humanity was the result of the Lord God's initiative and action. The passage may not say exactly how he gave life to mankind, but it does say that he is the one who gave the breath of life to mankind.

The gift of food. The Lord God made a garden for the man to live in which had abundant fruit trees for his food. The second gift to mankind was plenty of food to sustain life.[18] Hill (2000) argues that the Garden of Eden was a historical place located near the head of the Persian Gulf. She correlates the terrain with the description in our passage. The name *Eden*[19] means delight (Sailhamer, 2008, p. 75). It was a delightful place for the man to meet with the Lord God and to walk and talk with Him.[20]

"No **mankind** to cultivate the ground"[21] refers to the lack of farmers. This implies that the Lord God provided food for mankind before there was agriculture.

The gift of a helper. The third gift to mankind was a helper for the man.[22] The man gave names to domesticated animals, birds, and wild animals.[23] None was a suitable partner. Mankind is not like the animals. He is like God in certain limited ways.[24] Therefore, a special partner was necessary. The passage uses the image of a surgeon ("took one of his ribs" (NASB)[25]) to describe giving the man a wife. The details are not explained. A traditional interpretation assumes this is like a TV news story. Like the image of the potter above, I interpret the image of the surgeon figuratively. The focus is on the material that the wife was made of—the same stuff as the man—rather than how the Lord God did it.

The passage emphasizes that husband and wife are similar to each other[26] and different from the animals.[27] They should have mutual care for each other. Together the husband and wife can worship and obey the Lord God better than

---

[17]2:4–7.
[18]2:8–17.
[19]2:8.
[20]3:8–9.
[21]2:5. 3:17–18 is the first mention of agriculture.
[22]2:18–24.
[23]2:20.
[24]1:27.
[25]2:21–22.
[26]2:23.
[27]2:20.

they can individually. The end result was a man and a woman, married to each other.

> And be subject to one another in the fear of Christ. ... Nevertheless, each individual among you also is to love his own wife even as himself, and the wife must see to it that she respects her husband.
>
> Ephesians 5:21–33 (NASB)

Dignity

Read Genesis 2:7.

And do not suppose that you can say to yourselves, "We have Abraham for our father"; for I say to you that from these stones God is able to raise up children to Abraham.
Matthew 3:9 (NASB)

Is having monkeys for ancestors insulting? Some people think that having a famous ancestor bestows dignity on a person. Aristocrats are proud of their heritage. In Jesus' day, the Jews thought having Abraham as an ancestor made them special. In response, John the Baptist told them stones could be descendants of Abraham—not very special.

Maybe ancestry is not very important after all. Jesus taught that one's actions and attitudes are what are important. The fact that God loves mankind is the true source of dignity. My origin was in the heart of the Lord. His love for me is the basis for my self-respect.

PRAYER: Lord, thank you for creating me and giving me your dignity. Because you love me, I can love myself and then love others. Amen.

5

Are people naturally good?

I, the Lord, search the heart,
I test the mind,
Even to give to each man according to his ways,
According to the results of his deeds.

Jeremiah 17:10 (NASB)

In the ancient Greek story of Pandora's Box, a maiden named Pandora opened a forbidden box, and suddenly, evil entered the world. The pagan Greek worldview has been very influential on Western civilization. Some interpret Adam and Eve's sin like Pandora's Box, as though evil is something almost tangible that was released by Eve's action. Are Adam and Eve responsible for sin? What does the Bible say?

Genesis 2:25–3:24 (NASB)

C. FALL

1. Sin against God

25 And the man and his wife were both naked and were not ashamed.

CHAPTER 3

1 Now the serpent was more crafty than any beast of the field which the Lord God had made. And he said to the **wife**, "Indeed, has God said, 'You shall not eat from any tree of the garden'?"

2 The **wife** said to the serpent, "From the fruit of the trees of the garden we may eat; 3 but from the fruit of the tree which is in the middle of the garden, God has said, 'You shall not eat from it or touch it, or you will die.' "

4 The serpent said to the **wife**, "You surely will not die! 5 For God knows that in the day you eat from it your eyes will be opened, and you will be like God, knowing good and evil."

6 When the **wife** saw that the tree was good for food, and that it was a delight to the eyes, and that the tree was desirable to make one wise, she took from its fruit and ate; and she gave also to her husband with her, and he ate. 7 Then the eyes of both of them were opened, and they knew that they were naked; and they sewed fig leaves together and made themselves loin coverings.

2. Judgment

8 They heard the sound of the Lord God walking in the garden in the cool of the day, and the man and his wife hid themselves from the presence of the Lord God among the trees of the garden.

9 Then the Lord God called to the man, and said to him, "Where are you?"

10 He said, "I heard the sound of You in the garden, and I was afraid because I was naked; so I hid myself."

11 And He said, "Who told you that you were naked? Have you eaten from the tree of which I commanded you not to eat?"

12 The man said, "The **wife** whom You gave to be with me, she gave me from the tree, and I ate."

13 Then the Lord God said to the **wife**, "What is this you have done?"

And the **wife** said, "The serpent deceived me, and I ate."

14 The Lord God said to the serpent,

"Because you have done this,
Cursed are you more than all cattle,
And more than every beast of the field;
On your belly you will go,
And dust you will eat
All the days of your life;
15 And I will put enmity
Between you and the **wife**,
And between your seed and her seed;
He shall bruise you on the head,
And you shall bruise him on the heel."

16 To the **wife** He said,

"I will greatly multiply
Your pain in childbirth,
In pain you will bring forth children;
Yet your desire will be for your husband,
And he will rule over you."

17 Then to Adam He said, "Because you have listened to the

voice of your wife, and have eaten from the tree about which I commanded you, saying, 'You shall not eat from it';

> Cursed is the ground because of you;
> In toil you will eat of it
> All the days of your life.
> 18 Both thorns and thistles it shall grow for you;
> And you will eat the plants of the field;
> 19 By the sweat of your face
> You will eat bread,
> Till you return to the ground,
> Because from it you were taken;
> For you are dust,
> And to dust you shall return."

20 Now the man called his wife's name Eve, because she was the mother of all the living.

3. Protection

21 The Lord God made garments of skin for Adam and his wife, and clothed them.

22 Then the Lord God said,

> "Behold, the man has become like one of Us, knowing good and evil; and now, he might stretch out his hand, and take also from the tree of life, and eat, and live forever"

23 —therefore the Lord God sent him out from the garden of Eden, to cultivate the ground from which he was taken. 24 So He drove the man out; and at the east of the garden of Eden He stationed the cherubim and the flaming sword which turned every direction to guard the way to the tree of life.

The Fall is the traditional name for the story of the first sin in the Bible.[1] The beginning of the story is marked by literary connections. *Naked* (NASB)[2] and *crafty* (NASB)[3] is wordplay in Hebrew. This pair of words links the last verse in chapter 2 with the beginning of chapter 3, so I conclude that they are in the same section (Sailhamer, 2008, pp. 83–84).

The first section of the story is framed by the explanation of their nakedness in 2:25 and 3:7. *Crafty* (NASB)[4] means wise and is not a negative quality (Sailhamer, 2008, p. 84). This word connects 3:1 with the word *wise* (NASB) in 3:6. This adds to the literary symmetry of the first section of the story. The end of

---

[1] 2:25–3:24.
[2] 2:25. The Hebrew word *'arom* (Strong's No. 6174).
[3] 3:1. The Hebrew word *'arum* (Strong's No. 6175).
[4] 3:1.

the second section[5] is marked by poetry[6] and a narrative epilogue.[7] The third section[8] marks the end of the story of the Fall with a statement by the Lord God[9] followed by a narrative epilogue.[10]

Like the second chapter of Genesis, the story of the Fall consistently uses the name the *Lord God*[11] combining his personal name and his title as Creator.

Knowledge[12] is the same word as the Hebrew euphemism for sexual intimacy. Thus, knowing evil intimately through experience is not desirable.[13] The phrase "you will surely die" (NASB) in 2:17 is a judicial sentence of death, not a statement of cause and effect (Sailhamer, 2008, p. 82).

My outline of Genesis 3 has common features with several other stories.

1. Sin occurs.

2. God judges the sin.

3. God provides protection from the consequences.

4. In some stories, God provides restoration and a blessing.

In the story of the Fall, the man and his wife sinned against the Lord God by directly disobeying his command. In the story of Cain and Abel,[14] Cain sinned against his brother by murdering him. In the story of the Flood,[15] people corrupted the land, but God protected Noah and his family. In the story of Noah's Curse,[16] Ham dishonored his father. In the story of the Tower of Babel,[17] the builders challenged the authority of God. Each of these stories illustrates a different kind of sin and the corresponding judgment and mercy.

Are people naturally good?

Dr. Benjamin Spock's influential book (1946) on parenting assumes that children are good. The book makes excuses for sinful behavior, and claims that guilty feelings are unhealthy. It is assumed that children misbehave because adults do not treat them right. The underlying assumption is that one's environment is the source of corruption and sin. Such ideas are widespread in modern culture. Are people naturally good?

---

[5]3:8–20.
[6]3:17–19
[7]3:20.
[8]3:21–24.
[9]3:22.
[10]3:23–24.
[11]The Hebrew word *yhwh* (*Strong's* No. 3068). The Hebrew word *'elohim* (*Strong's* No. 430).
[12]2:9.
[13]See also 3:6.
[14]4:1–26.
[15]6:5–9:17.
[16]9:18–27.
[17]11:1–9.

At the end of the sixth day of Creation, God said that all creation, including mankind, was very good.[18] Therefore, are not people naturally good?

The Lord God's plan was a voluntary love-relationship with mankind—a very good thing. The Lord was seeking relationship with the man and his wife in the garden. The man and his wife could have obeyed the Lord God's command and could have continued to experience that very good thing. Creation was very good. However, the ability to disobey is a necessary ingredient of a voluntary relationship. The man and his wife chose to disobey.

The story of the Fall shows us the connection between sin and the judicial sentence of death.[19] The snake and the man and his wife are representative of Satan and all mankind, respectively. The curses[20] apply to all who act like them. Deception is typical of Satan, and disobedience is typical of mankind. We all sin from an early age and thus, deserve the death that comes to all, but Jesus paid the penalty for our sins, so that we can receive righteousness and life from him.

Paul quotes Psalms 14:1–3 and other Old Testament Scriptures, when he says, "There is none righteous, no, not one . . ."[21] The psalmist David said, "Behold, I was brought forth in iniquity, And in sin my mother conceived me."[22] David did not think that cute little babies are sinless. No, people are not naturally good.

> For there is no distinction; for all have sinned and fall short of the glory of God, being justified as a gift by His grace through the redemption which is in Christ Jesus;
>
> Romans 3:22–24 (NASB)

Who is responsible for sin?

Even though the goodness question is settled, the question remains, "Who is responsible for sin?" The answer hinges on how one interprets a passage in Romans.

> Therefore, just as through one man sin entered into the world, and death through sin, and so death spread to all men because all sinned . . . So then as through one transgression there resulted condemnation to all men, even so through one act of righteousness there resulted justification of life to all men. For as through the one man's disobedience the many were made sinners, even so through the obedience of the One the many will be made righteous.
>
> Romans 5:12–19 (NASB)

---

[18] 1:31.
[19] 2:17.
[20] 3:14–19.
[21] Romans 3:10,ff. (KJV).
[22] Psalms 51:5 (NASB).

The traditional interpretation of Romans 5:19 claims that the sinful nature is transmitted to all humanity by genetic inheritance[23]—the doctrine of Original Sin. Clouser (2016) and McIntyre (2002) explain that clear formulation of this interpretation dates from St. Augustine (about AD 400).[24] I'm uncomfortable with the similarity between the doctrine of Original Sin and the story of Pandora's Box. I wonder if pagan Greek and Roman culture was too influential in AD 400. I'm not an expert theologian, so an in-depth discussion of the doctrine of Original Sin is beyond the scope of this book, but the following are a few observations.

The doctrine of Original Sin is not explicitly stated in Romans 5. Romans 5:19 does not explain the mechanism that made all mankind sinners, but it does draw a comparison between Adam and Christ. Romans 5 attributes the origin of sin to one historical man.[25] It also attributes redemption to one historical man, our Lord Jesus Christ. The man's disobedience in the Garden of Eden was a historical event,[26] just as Christ's obedience going to the cross was a historical event. The man's disobedience was the event that caused all such behavior to be considered sin. Christ's obedience at the cross caused righteousness to be imputed to mankind. The redeeming blood of Jesus is timeless and effective for those who lived by faith before Christ (BC) and after Christ (AD).[27] Similarly, the consequence of sin is timeless.[28]

The Lord God systematically questioned the man and his wife, and judged each one individually. This illustrates the general principle that each person is responsible for his own actions.[29]

> But each one is tempted when he is carried away and enticed by his own lust. Then when lust has conceived, it gives birth to sin; and when sin is accomplished, it brings forth death.
>
> James 1:14–15 (NASB)

The man in the garden was given a law, and he paid the price for his disobedience. Those who do not have law also pay the price for their sin.[30] Everyone is accountable for his own actions.

Someone might say, "Isn't that cute little baby innocent?" The Scriptures give a clear answer to the goodness question. People are not naturally good. The more important question to me is "Who is responsible for my sin?" Some

---

[23]3:20.

[24]Clouser (2016) disagrees with St. Augustine's interpretation of Romans 5. McIntyre (2006a) also proposes a reinterpretation of Romans 5 and the doctrine of the Fall. In the same issue of *Perspectives on Science and Christian Faith*, several authors critically respond to McIntyre's proposed interpretation (Hurd, 2006; Murphy, 2006; Wilcox, 2006; Yoder, 2006). McIntyre (2006b), in turn, replies to the responders. Taken as a whole, this set of articles is a good conversation about an important doctrine of the faith, presenting a variety of views.

[25]Genesis 3:17 is the first place where *'adam* appears to be the personal name Adam. Earlier verses refer to *the man*.

[26]3:6.

[27]Hebrews 11:13,39–40.

[28]Romans 6:23.

[29]Romans 1:18–20, Jeremiah 17:10, and Ezekiel 18:1–32.

[30]Romans 2:12.

would rather debate an abstract question than be confronted with personal responsibility. I am responsible for my own sin.

I don't think sin is just floating around in the gene pool. The Bible does not say that the sinful nature is genetically inherited, but the Bible does say that redemption from sin is available by faith through the blood of Jesus.

How to be happy

Read Genesis 3:4–7.

Delight yourself in the Lord;
And He will give you the desires of your heart.

Psalms 37:4 (NASB)

Everybody wants to be happy. You see many different strategies these days. Some people try to get rich. Some buy big toys. Some try to be famous. Some look for new thrills.

The serpent claimed that happiness is being like God. The wife thought that she could get wisdom without asking God for it. She forgot that mankind was already like God, and that the Lord freely gives wisdom to those who ask for it.

When the man and his wife were banished from the garden, they no longer were with God. The east entrance to the garden was blocked by an angel. Sin broke their relationship. True happiness is being with God.

PRAYER: Lord, I want to experience your presence every day. I know my happiness comes from being with you. Thank you for your wisdom for today's challenges. Amen.

6

Is revenge acceptable?

> You shall not take vengeance, nor bear any grudge against the sons
> of your people, but you shall love your neighbor as yourself; I am
> the Lord.
>
> Leviticus 19:18 (NASB)

If someone hurts me, my natural reaction is to retaliate and try to hurt him. I
quote the Bible, "An eye for an eye."[1] I rationalize, "I have a right to get even!"
If I am unable to exact revenge myself, I might call in reinforcements. A kid
might say, "My big brother will beat you up." An adult might say, "I'm suing
you. I'll see you in court." What does Genesis have to say about revenge?

Genesis 4:1–26 (NASB)

D. CAIN AND ABEL

1. Sin against Brother

CHAPTER 4

1 Now the man had relations with his wife Eve, and she conceived
and gave birth to Cain, and she said, "I have gotten a manchild
with the help of the Lord." 2 Again, she gave birth to his brother
Abel. And Abel was a keeper of flocks, but Cain was a tiller of the
ground.

3 So it came about in the course of time that Cain brought an
offering to the Lord of the fruit of the ground. 4 Abel, on his part
also brought of the firstlings of his flock and of their fat portions.
And the Lord had regard for Abel and for his offering; 5 but for
Cain and for his offering He had no regard. So Cain became very
angry and his countenance fell.

---

[1]Leviticus 24:20.

6 Then the Lord said to Cain, "Why are you angry? And why has your countenance fallen? 7 If you do well, will not your countenance be lifted up? And if you do not do well, sin is crouching at the door; and its desire is for you, but you must master it."

8 Cain told Abel his brother. And it came about when they were in the field, that Cain rose up against Abel his brother and killed him.

2. Judgment

9 Then the Lord said to Cain, "Where is Abel your brother?"

And he said, "I do not know. Am I my brother's keeper?"

10 He said, "What have you done? The voice of your brother's blood is crying to Me from the ground. 11 Now you are cursed from the ground, which has opened its mouth to receive your brother's blood from your hand. 12 When you cultivate the ground, it will no longer yield its strength to you; you will be a vagrant and a wanderer on the **land**."

13 Cain said to the Lord, "My **guilt** is too great to bear! 14 Behold, You have driven me this day from the face of the ground; and from Your face I will be hidden, and I will be a vagrant and a wanderer on the **land**, and whoever finds me will kill me."

3. Protection

15 So the Lord said to him, "Therefore whoever kills Cain, vengeance will be taken on him sevenfold." And the Lord appointed a sign for Cain, so that no one finding him would slay him.

16 Then Cain went out from the presence of the Lord, and settled in the land of Nod, east of Eden.

17 Cain had relations with his wife and she conceived, and gave birth to Enoch; and he built a city, and called the name of the city Enoch, after the name of his son.

18 Now to Enoch was born Irad, and Irad became the **ancestor** of Mehujael, and Mehujael became the **ancestor** of Methushael, and Methushael became the **ancestor** of Lamech.

19 Lamech took to himself two wives: the name of the one was Adah, and the name of the other, Zillah. 20 Adah gave birth to Jabal; he was the father of those who dwell in tents and have livestock. 21 His brother's name was Jubal; he was the father of all those who play the lyre and pipe. 22 As for Zillah, she also gave birth to Tubal-cain, the forger of all implements of bronze and iron; and the sister of Tubal-cain was Naamah. 23 Lamech said to his wives,

"Adah and Zillah,
Listen to my voice,
You wives of Lamech,
Give heed to my speech,
For I have killed a man for wounding me;

And a boy for striking me;
24 If Cain is avenged sevenfold,
Then Lamech seventy-sevenfold."

4. Restoration

25 Adam had relations with his wife again; and she gave birth to a son,

and named him Seth, for, she said, "God has appointed me another offspring in place of Abel, for Cain killed him."

26 To Seth, to him also a son was born;

and he called his name Enosh.

Then men began to call upon the name of the Lord.

Our outline for the story of Cain and Abel[2] follows a similar pattern as the story of the Fall:[3] (1) sin, (2) judgment, (3) protection, and (4) restoration. The final section concludes with the namings of Seth and Enosh[4] followed by a narrative sentence.[5]

The first section[6] tells about the birth of Cain and Abel. *Manchild* (NASB),[7] referring to Cain, emphasizes his masculinity. This section concludes with the murder of Abel.

The second section[8] tells about the Lord's judgment of Cain.

The third section[9] explains that the Lord protected Cain from an avenger. The third section is framed by the phrases *vengeance seven times over*[10] and *...seventy-seven times.*[11]

The final section[12] tells about the birth of Seth, who took Abel's place. *Seth* and *appointed* (NASB)[13] is wordplay in Hebrew (Sailhamer, 1990, p. 69). The final section mentions seven persons, namely, Adam, his wife, Seth, Abel, Cain, Enosh, and the Lord. Seven is associated with completeness, and so the set of seven names is a literary device that provides a sense of completion to the story of Adam's family.

---

[2] 4:1–26.
[3] 2:25–3:24.
[4] 4:25.
[5] 4:26.
[6] 4:1–8.
[7] 4:1. The Hebrew word *'ish* (*Strong's* No. 376).
[8] 4:9–14.
[9] 4:15–24.
[10] 4:15.
[11] 4:24.
[12] 4:25–26.
[13] 4:25.

The story of Cain and Abel uses the name *Lord*,[14] his personal name, rather than *God*[15] or *Lord God*,[16] because a personal relationship with him is more relevant here than his role as Creator.

There were seven patriarchs from Adam through Cain to Lamech,[17] indicating a complete genealogy. *Begat* (KJV) (*became the father of* (NASB))[18] is a broad word meaning *became the ancestor of* (Barker, 1995, *s.v.* 5:6 NIV text note). In genealogies, I translate it as **ancestor** rather than *father* (NASB).

Is revenge acceptable?

Kids on the playground understand revenge very well. If one kid insults another, an insult flies back. Pretty soon there is a lot of shouting and trash talk. If one kid shoves another, he gets shoved back. Pretty soon there is a no-holds-barred fight. In some neighborhoods, gangs kill each other for revenge, and innocent bystanders suffer. "Getting even" is a principle that kids learn from an early age. Is revenge acceptable?

Genesis tells the story of the first murder in the Bible. Evidently, Cain lured his brother to an isolated place. This indicates premeditated murder. Cain tried to hide his sin. He lied to the Lord. The Lord judged Cain for the murder of Abel. *Punishment* (NASB)[19] also means iniquity or guilt (Sailhamer, 2008, pp. 100–101). I translate it as **guilt** in verse 13. Cain recognized his guilt, and the Lord recognized Cain's repentance (Sailhamer, 2008, pp. 100–101).[20] Cain's punishment was banishment from the land. Banishment was common in ancient civilizations. For example, Moses had to go to the land of Midian for forty years, because he murdered an Egyptian. *Nod*[21] means wandering, so Cain left the land of his family and the land of the Lord's presence to go to the land of wandering.

Cain was worried that an avenger would kill him.[22] He thought that banishment would be equivalent to the death penalty. The Lord was merciful, because he provided Cain a protective sign to prevent a cycle of revenge.[23] Details about the sign are not explained.

Some commentators interpret everything about Cain and his descendants (Cain's race) in a negative way.[24] Sailhamer (2008, pp. 102–103) emphasizes the idea of refuge from revenge. Sailhamer argues that the city of Enoch was a prototype for the cities of refuge specified in the Law of Moses. Rather than

---

[14]The Hebrew word *yhwh* (*Strong's* No. 3068).

[15]1:1–2:3.

[16]2:4–3:24.

[17]4:17–18.

[18]4:17. The Hebrew word *yalad* (*Strong's* No. 3205).

[19]4:13. The Hebrew word *'awoni* (*Strong's* No. 5771).

[20]4:13–15.

[21]4:16. The Hebrew word *nod* (*Strong's* No. 5113).

[22]4:14.

[23]4:15.

[24]For example, *Matthew Henry's Commentary s.v.* 4:19–24.

looking at the stories in Genesis through a race-oriented prism, I prefer Sailhamer's approach. The story of Cain and Abel teaches that revenge is not the Lord's way. Only God has the right to vengeance. This is confirmed in the New Testament.

> Never pay back evil for evil to anyone. Respect what is right in the sight of all men. If possible, so far as it depends on you, be at peace with all men. Never take your own revenge, beloved, but leave room for the wrath of God, for it is written, "Vengeance is mine, I will repay," says the Lord.
>
> Romans 12:17–19 (NASB)

The Bible teaches that all sin deserves death, but human revenge is not applicable. From the Lord's eternal perspective, Jesus paid the death penalty for mankind. Revenge is not acceptable.

> For the wages of sin is death, but the free gift of God is eternal life in Christ Jesus our Lord.
>
> Romans 6:23 (NASB)

What style of worship is best?

There are many Christian denominations. Each has distinctive doctrines and traditions. Styles of worship differ from one congregation to another—elaborate, simple, traditional, contemporary, and so on. Each worships in a different way. The story of Cain and Abel poses the question, "What style of worship is best?"

Cain and Abel each worshiped the Lord differently. Cain offered farm produce, and Abel offered meat and fat from his flock. The Lord accepted Abel's offering, but rejected Cain's. How was Cain to know what kind of offering was acceptable?

When the Lord spoke to Cain,[25] it is clear that Cain knew the right thing to do, even though we are not told the details. The Lord was not judgmental about the offering. Cain could have made another offering that would have been acceptable. The Lord was not unfair to Cain.

According to the Law of Moses, an offering[26] may be any of a variety of items, including grain. Both types of offerings by Cain and Abel were acceptable in themselves (Sailhamer, 2008, p. 97). The type of offering was not the issue. Hebrews 11:4 explains that Abel made his offering in faith. Heart attitude was what mattered to the Lord.

Cain's reaction was jealousy, anger, and hatred. Too often Christians have felt the same way about fellow believers who worship differently. Jesus taught that hatred is equivalent to murder.[27] I might feel that my group is the only

---

[25] 4:6–7.
[26] 4:5. The Hebrew word *minhah* (*Strong's* No. 4503).
[27] Matthew 5:21–22.

one worshiping the so-called "biblical way." Whenever I feel animosity toward those whose customs seem strange, I must repent. Perhaps my own worship the so-called "biblical way" is corrupted by my attitude like Cain's offering was. Humility is the prerequisite to worshiping properly.

This story concludes with the simple statement, "Then men began to call upon the name of the Lord."[28] True worshipers know the Lord personally. A relationship with him has always been the key to true worship.

The story of Cain and Abel describes the first murder in the Bible. The Lord's mercy is why Cain received protection from an avenger. Avoiding revenge is important, but the question I confront each week is "What style of worship is best?" Some people like to debate this question pointing out all the liturgical differences among Christian groups. Abel is my example. He worshiped in faith. Jesus taught that worship in spirit and truth is best. Liturgical differences don't matter to me. I can treasure the truth expressed by them all.

> But an hour is coming, and now is, when the true worshipers will worship the Father in spirit and truth; for such people the Father seeks to be His worshipers. God is spirit, and those who worship Him must worship in spirit and truth.
>
> John 4:23–24 (NASB)

---

[28] 4:26..

Offended

Read Genesis 4:6–7.

Above all, maintain an intense love for each other, since love covers a multitude of sins.

1 Peter 4:8 (HCSB)

Hatred stirs up conflicts,
but love covers all offenses.

Proverbs 10:12 (HCSB)

The church member's feelings were hurt by something the pastor did. Family members took up the offense. A group left the church in protest. People often hold onto a grudge long after the original church member has forgiven and forgotten—a tragedy.

Disappointments in life can easily lead to jealousy and ultimately to hatred of others, which is equivalent to murder. Sin against my brother breaks my relationship with the Lord. Yet, even when I am far from the Lord, his mercy provides protection and refuge. The mercy of the Lord draws the offended to repentance and reconciliation.

PRAYER: Lord, I want to let go of anger quickly, so no bitterness takes root in my life. Help me to forgive the brother who is inconsiderate, even if he is the pastor. Amen.

7

How long did the patriarchs live?

> Therefore, since we have so great a cloud of witnesses surrounding us, let us also lay aside every encumbrance and the sin which so easily entangles us, and let us run with endurance the race that is set before us.
>
> Hebrews 12:1 (NASB)

Believers who have died before me are my examples, especially those who were my relatives. Some branches of my family tree are documented back more than two hundred years. The Christian legacy of forefathers can be inspiring.

Genesis includes genealogies about the descendants of Adam. Most of us would say that biblical genealogies are boring. We tend to skip over them, but some of the details are revealing. Enoch walked with God. Methuselah lived a long life. Noah obeyed the Lord and built an ark. What does Genesis say about Methuselah and the other patriarchs?

Genesis 5:1–6:4 (NASB)

E. GENEALOGY OF MANKIND

1. Title

CHAPTER 5

1 This is the **genealogy** of the generations of **mankind**.

In the day when God created **mankind**, He made him in the likeness of God. 2 He created them male and female, and He blessed them and named them **Mankind** in the day when they were created.

2. Sons

3 When Adam had lived one hundred and thirty years, he became the father of a son in his own likeness, according to his image, and named him Seth. 4 Then the days of Adam after he became the father of Seth were eight hundred years, and he had other sons and daughters. 5 So all the days that Adam lived were nine hundred and thirty years, and he died.

6 Seth lived one hundred and five years, and became the father of Enosh. 7 Then Seth lived eight hundred and seven years after he became the father of Enosh, and he had other sons and daughters. 8 So all the days of Seth were nine hundred and twelve years, and he died.

9 Enosh lived ninety years, and became the **ancestor** of Kenan. 10 Then Enosh lived eight hundred and fifteen years after he became the **ancestor** of Kenan, and he had other sons and daughters. 11 So all the days of Enosh were nine hundred and five years, and he died.

12 Kenan lived seventy years, and became the **ancestor** of Mahalalel. 13 Then Kenan lived eight hundred and forty years after he became the **ancestor** of Mahalalel, and he had other sons and daughters. 14 So all the days of Kenan were nine hundred and ten years, and he died.

15 Mahalalel lived sixty-five years, and became the **ancestor** of Jared. 16 Then Mahalalel lived eight hundred and thirty years after he became the **ancestor** of Jared, and he had other sons and daughters. 17 So all the days of Mahalalel were eight hundred and ninety-five years, and he died.

18 Jared lived one hundred and sixty-two years, and became the **ancestor** of Enoch. 19 Then Jared lived eight hundred years after he became the **ancestor** of Enoch, and he had other sons and daughters. 20 So all the days of Jared were nine hundred and sixty-two years, and he died.

21 Enoch lived sixty-five years, and became the **ancestor** of Methuselah. 22 Then Enoch walked with God three hundred years after he became the **ancestor** of Methuselah, and he had other sons and daughters. 23 So all the days of Enoch were three hundred and sixty-five years. 24 Enoch walked with God; and he was not, for God took him.

25 Methuselah lived one hundred and eighty-seven years, and became the **ancestor** of Lamech. 26 Then Methuselah lived seven hundred and eighty-two years after he became the **ancestor** of Lamech, and he had other sons and daughters. 27 So all the days of Methuselah were nine hundred and sixty-nine years, and he died.

28 Lamech lived one hundred and eighty-two years, and became the father of a son.

29 Now he called his name Noah, saying, "This one will

give us rest from our work and from the toil of our hands arising from the ground which the Lord has cursed."

30 Then Lamech lived five hundred and ninety-five years after he became the father of Noah, and he had other sons and daughters. 31 So all the days of Lamech were seven hundred and seventy-seven years, and he died.

32 Noah was five hundred years old, and Noah became the father of Shem, Ham, and Japheth.

3. Heroes

CHAPTER 6

1 Now it came about, when **mankind** began to multiply on the face of the land, and daughters were born to them, 2 that the sons of God saw that the daughters of **mankind** were beautiful; and they took wives for themselves, whomever they chose.

3 Then the Lord said,

"My Spirit shall not strive with **mankind** forever, because he also is flesh; nevertheless his days shall be one hundred and twenty years."

4 The Nephilim were on the **land** in those days, and also afterward, when the sons of God came in to the daughters of **mankind**, and they bore children to them. Those were the mighty men who were of old, men of renown.

The outline consists of a title, a genealogy, and an epilogue about the heroes of that era. The phrase Adam *named him Seth* (NASB)[1] matches the phrase Lamech *called his name Noah*, (NASB)[2] to frame the genealogy. The end of the genealogy section is marked by the naming of Noah and a few narrative verses.[3] Sailhamer (2008, pp. 105–106, 114–115) argues, based on literary form, that 6:1–4 is an epilogue to the prior genealogy, rather than the introduction to the Flood narrative. The end of the epilogue section is marked by God's statement[4] and a narrative verse.[5]

The Creator's title *God* (NASB)[6] is generally used in this passage, because he is identified as Creator in the first verse. However, *Lord* (NASB),[7] his personal name, is used in 5:29, rather than *God*, because Lamech's lament is about mankind's broken relationship with the Lord, rather than his role as Creator.

---

[1] 5:3.
[2] 5:29.
[3] 5:30–32.
[4] 6:3.
[5] 6:4.
[6] The Hebrew word *'elohim* (*Strong's* No. 430).
[7] The Hebrew word *yhwh* (*Strong's* No. 3068).

Similarly, *Lord* (NASB) is used in 6:3, because he was seeking fellowship with mankind.

In the genealogy section, *begat* (KJV)[8] (*became the father of* (NASB)) is a broad word meaning *became the ancestor of* (Barker, 1995, *s.v.* 5:6 NIV text note). In genealogies, I translate it as *became the **ancestor** of* rather than *became the father of* (NASB) unless the passage clearly indicates a direct parental relationship.

There is disagreement among scholars over the translation of *strive* (NASB) and the interpretation of 6:3 (Sailhamer, 2008, p. 115). Therefore, I avoid any doctrine based on this verse.

How long did the patriarchs live?

My grandparents all lived long lives. Both of my grandfathers and one grandmother lived past 90. My other grandmother lived to be 84. However, living more than a hundred years is very rare these days. The Bible says that Methuselah lived 969 years. That sounds impossible. Skeptics seize on this to ridicule the reliability of the Bible. They say, "How can you believe the Bible is true when it is obviously wrong?"

The traditional interpretation of the genealogy in Genesis 5 takes the years of the patriarchs literally, reflecting a newspaper mentality. When faced with the huge lifespans of the patriarchs, some commentators just say, "Things were different then," or "Those individuals were special," even though the passage does not say so. Many modern commentators ignore the large numbers. I find such approaches unsatisfying. The appendix presents speculation that the large numbers are symbolic. The passage does not explain why the lifespans were unusually long, and does not indicate that they are symbolic. I wish I had a good answer for skeptics, but I don't.

Who was mankind's father?

This genealogy does address the question "Who was mankind's father?" The traditional answer is Adam. Genesis 5:3 and Luke 3:38 make it clear that there was a historical person named Adam. Adam was the first man mentioned in the Bible. Was Adam the father of mankind?

Anthropologists have found human-like remains that are a couple of million years old, and remains of anatomically modern man that are over 100,000 years old. The stories in Genesis seem much more recent.

Fischer (1993) proposes that Adam was the first Covenant Man, rather than the first anatomically modern man. This view allows for a relatively recent date for Adam and locates him in southern Mesopotamia. Fischer's interpretation is admittedly speculative. The Scriptures don't say whether Adam was the first Covenant Man.

---

[8]5:6 (KJV). The Hebrew word *yalad* (*Strong's* No. 3205).

Genesis does not claim that the historical Adam was the first human. Genesis 2:7 does not say "the man" was the first one, and 2:5 merely says there was no one engaged in agriculture at that time. I do know that the historical Adam mentioned in 5:3 was created by God, but the Bible does not say whether Adam was the first anatomically modern human.

Genesis 5:1–2 summarizes the earlier story of the creation of mankind, male and female.[9] Verse 3 begins the genealogy with Adam. Luke's genealogy of the Messiah calls Adam "the son of God" (NASB).[10] As explained in Genesis 2, the Lord God was the ultimate source of mankind, including Adam. Genesis 5 does not say who, if anyone, preceded Adam, but it does say that, as Creator, the Lord God was mankind's father.

---

[9] 1:26–27, 2:4–24.
[10] Luke 3:38.

Patriarchs

Read Genesis 5:3–32.

Now faith is the reality of what is hoped for, the proof of what is not seen. For our ancestors won God's approval by it.

Hebrews 11:1–2 (HCSB)

Benjamin Allen (1789–1829) was rector of St. Paul's Episcopal Church in Philadelphia, Pennsylvania. He energetically established churches, published tracts, and preached the gospel. Benjamin begat John; John begat Milton M.; Milton M. begat Milton B.; Milton B. begat James; and James begat Edward. I think this genealogy is interesting, because the lives of my ancestors are vivid examples to me.

The genealogy in Genesis 5 gives some details about the patriarchs. Seth called on the name of the Lord. Like him, I am seeking such a close relationship with the Lord that I can call him by his personal name. Enoch walked with God. They were such close friends that Enoch did not die, but was taken by the Lord. Noah also walked with God. When the Lord gave him instructions for building the ark, Noah obeyed. Noah also preached righteousness to his generation. Each of these patriarchs are examples to me.

PRAYER: Lord, I want my faith to be strong like the patriarchs. I will worship you like Seth. I will obey like Noah. I want to be close to you like Enoch and Noah. Amen.

Part II

Noah

8

Did the Flood cover all of Planet Earth?

By faith Noah, being warned by God about things not yet seen, in reverence prepared an ark for the salvation of his household, by which he condemned the world, and became an heir of the righteousness which is according to faith.

Hebrews 11:7 (NASB)

After working in industry, I went back to school to become a teacher. For five years after graduation, I wondered where I would be allowed to teach. After looking down many dead ends, I got a teaching job which turned out to be God's landing place for me. Trusting God for a safe landing place is much wiser than trying to figure everything out myself while the water is rising.

Noah was looking for a safe landing place, too. What does the Bible say about the Flood?

Genesis 6:5–7:24 (NASB)

II. NOAH

A. CORRUPTION OF THE LAND

5 Then the Lord saw that the wickedness of **mankind** was great on the **land**, and that every intent of the thoughts of his heart was only evil continually. 6 The Lord was sorry that He had made **mankind** on the **land**, and He was grieved in His heart. 7 The Lord said,

> "I will blot out **mankind** whom I have created from the face of the land, from **mankind** to animals to creeping things and to birds of the sky; for I am sorry that I have made them."

8 But Noah found favor in the eyes of the Lord.

B. GENEALOGY OF NOAH

1. Title

9 This is the **genealogy** of the generations of Noah.

Noah was a righteous man, blameless in his time; Noah walked with God.

2. Sons

10 Noah became the father of three sons: Shem,Ham and Japheth.

C. FLOOD OF THE LAND

1. Sin against the Land

11 Now the **land** was corrupt in the sight of God, and the **land** was filled with violence. 12 God looked on the **land**, and behold, it was corrupt; for all flesh had corrupted their way upon the **land**.

13 Then God said to Noah, "The end of all flesh has come before Me; for the **land** is filled with violence because of them; and behold, I am about to destroy them with the **land**. 14 Make for yourself an ark of gopher wood; you shall make the ark with rooms, and shall cover it inside and out with pitch. 15 This is how you shall make it: the length of the ark three hundred cubits, its breadth fifty cubits, and its height thirty cubits. 16 You shall make a window for the ark, and finish it to a cubit from the top; and set the door of the ark in the side of it; you shall make it with lower, second, and third decks. 17 Behold, I, even I am bringing the flood of water upon the **land**, to destroy all flesh in which is the breath of life, from under **the sky**; everything that is on the **land** shall perish. 18 But I will establish My covenant with you; and you shall enter the ark—you and your sons and your wife, and your sons' wives with you. 19 And of every living thing of all flesh, you shall bring two of every kind into the ark, to keep them alive with you; they shall be male and female. 20 Of the birds after their kind, and of the animals after their kind, of every creeping thing of the ground after its kind, two of every kind will come to you to keep them alive. 21 As for you, take for yourself some of all food which is edible, and gather it to yourself; and it shall be for food for you and for them."

22 Thus Noah did; according to all that God had commanded him, so he did.

2. Judgment

CHAPTER 7

1 Then the Lord said to Noah, "Enter the ark, you and all your household, for you alone I have seen to be righteous before Me in

this time. 2 You shall take with you of every clean animal by sevens, a male and his female; and of the animals that are not clean two, a male and his female; 3 also of the birds of the sky, by sevens, male and female, to keep offspring alive on the face of all the **land**. 4 For after seven more days, I will send rain on the **land** forty days and forty nights; and I will blot out from the face of the land every living thing that I have made."

5 Noah did according to all that the Lord had commanded him.

6 Now Noah was six hundred years old when the flood of water came upon the **land**. 7 Then Noah and his sons and his wife and his sons' wives with him entered the ark because of the water of the flood. 8 Of clean animals and animals that are not clean and birds and everything that creeps on the ground, 9 there went into the ark to Noah by twos, male and female, as God had commanded Noah. 10 It came about after the seven days, that the water of the flood came upon the **land**. 11 In the six hundredth year of Noah's life, in the second month, on the seventeenth day of the month, on the same day all the fountains of the great deep burst open, and the floodgates of the sky were opened. 12 The rain fell upon the **land** for forty days and forty nights.

13 On the very same day Noah and Shem and Ham and Japheth, the sons of Noah, and Noah's wife and the three wives of his sons with them, entered the ark, 14 they and every beast after its kind, and all the cattle after their kind, and every creeping thing that creeps on the **land** after its kind, and every bird after its kind, all sorts of birds. 15 So they went into the ark to Noah, by twos of all flesh in which was the breath of life. 16 Those that entered, male and female of all flesh, entered as God had commanded him; and the Lord closed it behind him.

17 Then the flood came upon the **land** for forty days, and the water increased and lifted up the ark, so that it rose above the **land**. 18 The water prevailed and increased greatly upon the **land**, and the ark floated on the surface of the water. 19 The water prevailed more and more upon the **land**, so that all the high **hills** everywhere under the **sky** were covered. 20 The water prevailed fifteen cubits higher, and the **hills** were covered. 21 All flesh that moved on the **land** perished, birds and cattle and beasts and every swarming thing that swarms upon the **land**, and all mankind; 22 of all that was on the dry land, all in whose nostrils was the breath of the spirit of life, died. 23 Thus He blotted out every living thing that was upon the face of the land, from man to animals to creeping things and to birds of the sky, and they were blotted out from the **land**; and only Noah was left, together with those that were with him in the ark.

24 The water prevailed upon the **land** one hundred and fifty days.

In the outline, the end of the section on the corruption of the land is marked by God's statement[1] and a narrative verse.[2]

The genealogy of Noah is very brief. Ham was youngest of Noah's sons.[3] Translators of 10:21 do not agree on who was oldest, Japheth or Shem. (The NASB chose Shem.)

The outline of the story of the Flood is similar to other Genesis stories: sin, judgment, protection, restoration, blessing, and covenant. The section on the sin against the land is concluded by Noah's obedience. In chapters 7 and 8, the mentioned waiting periods are symmetric: 7 days, 7 days, 40 days, 150 days, 150 days, 40 days, 7 days, and 7 days.[4] This gives literary structure to the story (Sailhamer, 2008, p. 127). The judgment section covers the first half of these waiting periods.

The story of Noah uses both *God* and *Lord*.[5] In each case, the context emphasizes either his role as Creator or his relationship with mankind.

Did the Flood cover all of Planet Earth?

The traditional interpretation of the story says that the Flood covered all of Planet Earth. However, geological science has found no evidence of a global flood. Skeptics point to this as proof that the Bible is not true. Debates are organized for and against. Most of us are just confused.

Creation Science[6] opposes mainstream geology, pointing to Noah's Flood as the explanation for a wide variety of geologic features (Whitcomb & Morris, 1961). Many believers have embraced this as the Christian alternative to secular science. They do not realize that there are many Christian professionals in science who find Creation Science to be poor science, and thus, not credible (Numbers, 1992). This controversy has generated heated arguments and elaborate debates over the last half century, not only between Christians and secular scientists, but also among Christians in science. There has been a flood of books and articles arguing for various theories. This book does not address this controversy between mainstream science and Creation Science.

Did the Flood cover all of Planet Earth? The key issue is whether the word **land**[7] should be interpreted as Planet Earth or a local area. Let us consider several related questions about details in the story.

Was the size of the ark too big for a wooden craft?   A cubit was about 18 inches in Israel around 1000 BC. No one is sure exactly how long a cubit was for Noah or Moses. Based on 18 inches per cubit, the ark was two and a half times

---

[1] 6:7.
[2] 6:8.
[3] 9:24.
[4] 7:4, 7:10, 7:12,17, 7:24, 8:3, 8:6, 8:10, and 8:12.
[5] The Hebrew word *'elohim* (*Strong's* No. 430). The Hebrew word *yhwh* (*Strong's* No. 3068).
[6] For example, as advocated by the Institute for Creation Research, http://www.icr.org/
[7] The Hebrew word *'eres* (*Strong's* No. 776).

the size of ancient Mediterranean ships and larger than the largest wooden ships of the modern era (Sailhamer, 2008, p.120). One might challenge whether such a large craft would be practical. However, China (c. AD 1400) had wooden ships larger than the ark (Cotterell, 1988, p. 127). Moreover, Noah's ark did not have to sail anywhere; it just had to float in a stable position without breaking apart. Thus, the literal size was not too big for a wooden craft.

Was the ark big enough for a global flood?   If the Flood covered Planet Earth, then Noah would have needed to fit all animal species into the ark plus enough food for them all for a year. Five categories of creatures were in the ark: domesticated animals, wild animals, creepers, birds, and mankind.[8] Given the dimensions of the ark, it was too small to hold all the species on Planet Earth in these categories. This is evidence that all kinds of animals in a limited locality were intended.

Was the water higher than Mount Everest?   Genesis says that all the "mountains" (NASB)[9] were covered by the flood waters. *Mountain* (NASB) can also be translated *hill* or *temple-tower* (C. A. Hill, 2002). I use **hill** consistently which is more appropriate for Mesopotamia. Perhaps, local hills were intended.

What does geologic data say?   Tanner (1996) argues that a single global flood cannot account for the geologic data, in contrast to Creation Science. For example, Seely (2003) summarizes data from the GISP2 ice core which was extracted from the Greenland ice sheet. It shows 110,000 annual layers of snow. This is strong evidence that there was no flood which covered Greenland at any time in the last 110,000 years. This is evidence that the Flood did not cover Planet Earth.

Where did Noah's ark land?   There have been several highly publicized expeditions to Mount Ararat in Turkey to find Noah's ark.[10]   However, *Ararat* (NASB)[11] in ancient times did not refer to the modern Mount Ararat in Turkey; the name referred to the region of Urartu in modern southeastern Turkey. Hill (2002) favors the vicinity of Jabel Judi, near Cizre, Turkey, as the most likely landing place of the ark.[12] Her opinion is consistent with a local tradition in that region. I do not know where Noah's ark landed.

---

[8]7:14.

[9]7:19–20. The Hebrew word *har* (*Strong's* No. 2022).

[10]Several such expeditions that claimed to have found the ark were later shown to be hoaxes (C. A. Hill, 2002).

[11]8:4.

[12]Carol Hill (2006) speculates on how the Flood could have occurred, and supports her theory with a qualitative analysis of the hydrology of the Tigris and Euphrates watershed, accompanied by a quantitative analysis by Alan Hill (2006).

Was the Flood just a myth? No, the New Testament teaches that Noah's Flood was a historical event.[13] Hill (2002) argues that the Flood was a local event in Mesopotamia, based on biblical exegesis and geologic evidence.

From the above considerations, I conclude that the Flood was a local catastrophe that destroyed all the inhabited land known to Noah. Perhaps the Flood's waters stretched from horizon to horizon, "everywhere under the **sky**" (NASB),[14] covering all the local hills and temple-towers.

Genesis 8:1–9:17 (NASB)

---

3. Protection

CHAPTER 8

1 But God remembered Noah and all the beasts and all the cattle that were with him in the ark; and God caused a wind to pass over the **land**, and the water subsided. 2 Also the fountains of the deep and the floodgates of the sky were closed, and the rain from the sky was restrained; 3 and the water receded steadily from the **land**, and at the end of one hundred and fifty days the water decreased. 4 In the seventh month, on the seventeenth day of the month, the ark rested upon the **hills** of Ararat. 5 The water decreased steadily until the tenth month; in the tenth month, on the first day of the month, the tops of the **hills** became visible.

4. Restoration

6 Then it came about at the end of forty days, that Noah opened the window of the ark which he had made; 7 and he sent out a raven, and it flew here and there until the water was dried up from the **land**. 8 Then he sent out a dove from him, to see if the water was abated from the face of the land; 9 but the dove found no resting place for the sole of her foot, so she returned to him into the ark, for the water was on the surface of all the **land**. Then he put out his hand and took her, and brought her into the ark to himself. 10 So he waited yet another seven days; and again he sent out the dove from the ark. 11 The dove came to him toward evening, and behold, in her beak was a freshly picked olive leaf. So Noah knew that the water was abated from the **land**. 12 Then he waited yet another seven days, and sent out the dove; but she did not return to him again.

13 Now it came about in the six hundred and first year, in the first month, on the first of the month, the water was dried up from the **land**. Then Noah removed the covering of the ark, and looked,

---

[13]For example, Matthew 24:37–39 and 2 Peter 3:5–6.
[14]7:19.

and behold, the surface of the ground was dried up. 14 In the second month, on the twenty-seventh day of the month, the **land** was dry.

15 Then God spoke to Noah, saying, 16 "Go out of the ark, you and your wife and your sons and your sons' wives with you. 17 Bring out with you every living thing of all flesh that is with you, birds and animals and every creeping thing that creeps on the **land**, that they may breed abundantly on the **land**, and be fruitful and multiply on the **land**."

18 So Noah went out, and his sons and his wife and his sons' wives with him. 19 Every beast, every creeping thing, and every bird, everything that moves on the **land**, went out by their families from the ark.

20 Then Noah built an altar to the Lord, and took of every clean animal and of every clean bird and offered burnt offerings on the altar. 21 The Lord smelled the soothing aroma; and the Lord said to Himself, "I will never again curse the ground on account of **mankind**, for the intent of **mankind**'s heart is evil from his youth; and I will never again destroy every living thing, as I have done.

22 While the **land** remains,
Seedtime and harvest,
And cold and heat,
And summer and winter,
And day and night
Shall not cease."

5. Blessing

CHAPTER 9

1 And God blessed Noah and his sons and said to them,

"Be fruitful and multiply, and fill the **land**. 2 The fear of you and the terror of you will be on every beast of the **land** and on every bird of the sky; with everything that creeps on the ground, and all the fish of the sea, into your hand they are given. 3 Every moving thing that is alive shall be food for you; I give all to you, as I gave the green plant. 4 Only you shall not eat flesh with its life, that is, its blood. 5 Surely I will require your lifeblood; from every beast I will require it. And from every man, from every man's brother I will require the life of **mankind**.

6 Whoever sheds **mankind**'s blood,
By **mankind** his blood shall be shed,
For in the image of God He made **mankind**.

7 As for you, be fruitful and multiply; Populate the **land** abundantly and multiply in it."

6. Covenant

8 Then God spoke to Noah and to his sons with him, saying, 9 "Now behold, I Myself do establish My covenant with you, and with your descendants after you; 10 and with every living creature that is with you, the birds, the cattle, and every beast of the **land** with you; of all that comes out of the ark, even every beast of the **land**. 11 I establish My covenant with you; and all flesh shall never again be cut off by the water of the flood, neither shall there again be a flood to destroy the **land**." 12 God said,

> "This is the sign of the covenant which I am making between Me and you and every living creature that is with you, for all successive generations; 13 I set My bow in the cloud, and it shall be for a sign of a covenant between Me and the **land**. 14 It shall come about, when I bring a cloud over the **land**, that the bow will be seen in the cloud, 15 and I will remember My covenant, which is between Me and you and every living creature of all flesh; and never again shall the water become a flood to destroy all flesh. 16 When the bow is in the cloud, then I will look upon it, to remember the everlasting covenant between God and every living creature of all flesh that is on the **land**."

17 And God said to Noah, "This is the sign of the covenant which I have established between Me and all flesh that is on the **land**."

The section on protection covers the 150 day waiting period. The section on restoration covers the remaining waiting periods of 40 days, 7 days, and 7 days, and its end is denoted by God's promise in poetry. Genesis 9:1 and 9:7 frame the blessing section, and the end of the section is marked by poetry and a narrative sentence.[15] The word *covenant* is repeated several times in the Covenant section[16] denoting its beginning and end.

Does God keep his promises?

The story of the Flood reveals something about God's character. The deeper question is "Does God keep his promises?"

Knowledge of good and evil[17] in the Garden of Eden degenerated into utter corruption in the time of Noah.[18] The Lord regretted making mankind, so he decided to wipe the land clean. If things were so bad, why was Noah saved?

---

[15] 9:6–7.
[16] 9:8-17.
[17] 3:5.
[18] 6:5.

Noah obeyed God over and over.[19] Noah walked with God, similar to Enoch.[20] The emphasis of the story is on salvation,[21] not judgment. God saved Noah and his family, because Noah and God walked together. Even though mankind had corrupted the land, the Lord still wanted fellowship with mankind.[22]

The blessings of Noah and of the land renewed earlier blessings given to creation. Genesis 9:1 is a renewal of the first blessing of creation, and Genesis 9:2 is a renewal of the second blessing of creation.[23] Genesis 9:5 is a renewal of the accounting required of Cain.[24] The Lord did not change his mind about these things.

Before the Flood, God promised to make a covenant with Noah.[25] As we have seen, Noah was obedient. The sign of the rainbow in the sky is the guarantee of God's promise. Faithfulness is a fundamental quality of his character. God keeps his promises.

---

[19] 6:22, 7:5, 7:13, and 8:18.
[20] 6:9.
[21] 7:23.
[22] 3:8.
[23] 1:28.
[24] 4:9.
[25] 6:18.

Comfort

Read Genesis 6:6–8.

Who shall separate us from the love of Christ? Shall trouble
or hardship or persecution or famine or nakedness or dan-
ger or sword? ...No, in all these things we are more than
conquerors through him who loved us.

Romans 8:35–37 (NIV)

Joan was in critical condition in the hospital due to cancer. We were
praying earnestly for her recovery. The Scriptures say that she is "more
than a conqueror." In the early morning hours, while Angie was with
her mother, Joan passed into the arms of her savior. As Angie left the
hospital in the dawn's light, she was grief-stricken and confused. Then
she saw a rainbow. She remembered that God keeps his promises.

God has feelings. He regretted that he made mankind, but Noah
comforted God when he was grieved. Noah was upright when no one
else was. Whenever I go through brokenness, I know that the Lord has
experienced the same grief and pain, and even more so. He knows how
to comfort the grieving.

PRAYER: Lord, thank you for comforting me when I faced
loss and disappointment. I will be careful to comfort others
whenever needed. Amen.

9

Does Noah's curse justify racial prejudice?

For though I am free from all men, I have made myself a slave to all, so that I may win more.

1 Corinthians 9:19 (NASB)

In an 1860 speech in the U.S. Congress, Jefferson Davis[1] invoked Genesis 9 as support for slavery (Haynes, 2002).

[When] the low and vulgar son of Noah, who laughed at his father's exposure, sunk by debasing himself and his lineage by a connection with an inferior race of men, he doomed his descendants to perpetual slavery.

Davis was referring to the then popular interpretation that Africans were descendants of Ham, and thus, that the slavery of Africans in the American South had divine approval. What does the Bible say?

Genesis 9:18–29 (NASB)

D. NOAH'S CURSE

1. Sons

18 Now the sons of Noah who came out of the ark were Shem and Ham and Japheth; and Ham was the father of Canaan. 19 These three were the sons of Noah, and from these the whole **land** was populated.

2. Sin Against Father

---

[1]Jefferson Davis became president of the Confederacy during the Civil War (1861–1865).

20 Then Noah began farming and planted a vineyard. 21 He drank of the wine and became drunk, and uncovered himself inside his tent. 22 Ham, the father of Canaan, saw the nakedness of his father, and told his two brothers outside. 23 But Shem and Japheth took a garment and laid it upon both their shoulders and walked backward and covered the nakedness of their father; and their faces were turned away, so that they did not see their father's nakedness.

3. Judgment

24 When Noah awoke from his wine, he knew what his youngest son had done to him. 25 So he said,

> "Cursed be Canaan;
> A servant of servants
> He shall be to his brothers."

26 He also said,

> "Blessed be the Lord,
> The God of Shem;
> And let Canaan be his servant.
> 27 May God enlarge Japheth,
> And let him dwell in the tents of Shem;
> And let Canaan be his servant."

E. GENEALOGY OF MANKIND COMPLETED

28 Noah lived three hundred and fifty years after the flood. 29 So all the days of Noah were nine hundred and fifty years, and he died.

The outline of the story of Noah's Curse is similar to other stories in Genesis, beginning with sin, followed by judgment. The end of the section is marked by poetry[2] and the narrative epilogue about Noah.[3]

Each patriarch of the Genealogy of Mankind[4] lived a certain number of years "and then he died." This phrase is missing for Noah in chapter 5. Genesis 9:28–29 completes the formula for Noah, and thus, completes the Genealogy of Mankind (Sailhamer, 2008, p. 110).

Does Noah's curse justify racial prejudice?

Growing up in the South in the 1960s, I was aware that some conservative Christians interpreted this passage from a racial perspective to justify their prejudice against African Americans. Based on 10:6, they thought that black

---

[2] 9:25–27.
[3] 9:28–29.
[4] 5:3–32.

Africans descended from Ham through Cush, and that because of Ham's sin against his father, his lineage is cursed. As I studied American history, the evil of slavery and racial prejudice was obvious. I wondered about this interpretation. Does Noah's curse justify racial prejudice?

Goldenberg (2005) traces in detail how this interpretation has very ancient origins, beginning with Jewish rabbis as early as 800 BC, continuing with the early church fathers, and even early Muslim commentators. It was a well established interpretation by the time Africans were enslaved in large numbers by Europeans from AD 1500 on.

Noah's curse was used to justify slavery of Africans in America as early as the 1670s (Haynes, 2002, p. 181).[5] A racial interpretation was so widespread in colonial America that early abolitionists felt compelled to argue against it (Haynes, 2002, p. 181). On the other hand, besides preachers from antebellum slave states, some respected Bible commentators provided supporting interpretations.

The English Bible expositor Matthew Henry (1662–1714) was well-respected in America. (His compact commentary is still widely read today.) His commentary on Genesis 9 emphasizes honor and shame, for example saying, "It is very wrong, ... to publish the faults of any, especially of parents, whom it is our duty to honour" (Henry, 1991, s.v. 9:18–23).

Adam Clarke's influential commentary, published between 1817 and 1825, also emphasizes honor and shame (Haynes, 2002, p.40).

> Ham, and very probably his son Canaan, had treated their father on this occasion with contempt or reprehensible levity. ... God had wise and powerful reasons to induce [Noah] to sentence the one to perpetual servitude, and to allot to the others prosperity and dominion. Besides, the curse pronounced on Canaan neither fell immediately upon himself nor on his worthless father, but upon the Canaanites; and from the history we have of this people, ... we may ask, "Could the curse of God fall more deservedly on any people than on these?" Their profligacy was great, but it was not the effect of the curse; but, being foreseen by the Lord, the curse was the effect of their conduct. (Clarke, 1996, s.v. 9:22–24)

Even though Henry and Clarke did not identify the curse with Africans, honor and shame resonated with Southern values in the antebellum period (Haynes, 2002, p. 39). Southerners, who had a low view of their slaves, readily associated the shameful conduct of Ham with all Africans.

After the Civil War, race receded into the background of mainstream interpretations of the story, but it reemerged during debates over segregation in the 1950s and 1960s (Haynes, 2002, p. 116). For example, during the Senate filibuster of the 1964 Civil Rights Act, Senator Robert Byrd said, "Noah apparently saw fit to discriminate against Ham's descendants in that he placed a

---

[5]Haynes' book, *Noah's Curse: The biblical Justification of American Slavery* is my primary source of information in this chapter.

curse upon Canaan" (Haynes, 2002, p. 116). This illustrates how the story was widely used in that era as evidence of divine approval for racial discrimination and segregation. *Dake's Annotated Reference Bible*, published in 1963, considers Noah's curse to be a "prophecy of a servile posterity from Ham" (Dake, 1963, s.v. 9:25). Moreover, his other notes on the passage have a racial frame of reference. (Dake, 1963, s.v. 9:25–27). Such commentary in this popular reference Bible bolstered segregationists in the 1960s (Haynes, 2002, p. 118).

From the 1830s on, abolitionists published extensively to discredit a racial interpretation of the passage (Haynes, 2002, p. 181). The same points are supported by modern commentators as well. Among their points were these.

- Ancient slavery was not analogous to the American institution in many respects (Jeffers, 1999). For example, it was not racially based. Moreover, ancient slavery was generally a temporary condition.

- Africans did not descend from Canaan and Ham was not cursed.

- The passage does not say that Noah had divine authority.

- Noah's pronouncement was not a curse, but rather a prediction. For example, Clarke (see above) and Sailhamer (2008, p. 135) argue that a proper translation of Noah's curse is a prediction, not a malediction (curse). The action of Ham foreshadowed later generations, such as the depravity of Canaanite worship in the time of Moses.

- The curse was fulfilled when the Israelites enslaved the Canaanites in the time of Joshua.

It is clear that the story does not imply that God approves of slavery or racial prejudice. The enslaving of Africans by Europeans was a great evil that has had terrible repercussions down to the present day.

Although the Bible takes slavery for granted as a part of ancient secular society, it teaches godly ethics in that context. For example,

- The Law of Moses protected slaves from abuse.[6]

- Masters must treat their slaves well.[7]

- Slaves must serve their masters faithfully.[8]

- Slaves should take advantage of the opportunity to be free.[9]

- Brothers dwelling in unity is ideal.[10]

- In the Body of Christ, there is no slave or free from God's perspective.[11]

---

[6]For example, Exodus 23:12 and Leviticus 25:39–43.
[7]Ephesians 6:9.
[8]Ephesians 6:5–8.
[9]1 Corinthians 7:21.
[10]Psalms 133:1 and John 13:34–35.
[11]Galatians 3:28

The Bible as a whole does not advocate the institution of slavery. In fact, biblical principles make slaveholding and underlying racist attitudes repugnant to Christians.

A skeptic might claim that the Bible is hopelessly out of date, because it was used to justify slavery. Genesis does not justify slavery of Ham's descendants nor prejudice toward them, and this interpretation has become only a historical footnote among Christians today. Noah's curse does not justify racial prejudice.

How can one honor others?

Shem and Japheth are examples of how to honor someone else. They discreetly covered the embarrassment of their father. The Apostle Paul told the Roman Christians to honor one another unselfishly because of their love for each other.[12] Of course, those around me are not perfect and may do something offensive. I must be careful not to gossip about their failings.[13] I must let love cover an offense instead of letting bitterness fester into hatred.[14]

> Hatred stirs up strife,
> But love covers all transgressions.
>
> Proverbs 10:12 (NASB)

---

[12] Romans 12:10.
[13] Proverbs 17:9.
[14] Hebrews 12:15.

A slave

Read Genesis 9:24–26.

> But thanks be to God that though you were slaves of sin, you became obedient from the heart to that form of teaching to which you were committed, and having been freed from sin, you became slaves of righteousness.
>
> Romans 6:17–18 (NASB)

Institutional slavery in modern society is not an issue for us. The deeper questions are "Am I a slave to natural desires? Money? Ambitions? Success? How can a person be free?" When I look at my natural inclinations, I realize that I could have been a bitter cynic. The natural me enjoys clever jokes that cut others to ribbons. Every news report exposes the foolishness of leaders, providing fuel for my bitterness. But because of God's grace, I am free from those natural self-destructive tendencies.

All were slaves to sin, but believers have been set free by Christ to live for God. As Christ's slave, I am free to forgive the weaknesses of others. As Christ's slave, I am free to humble myself with everyone I meet. As Christ's slave, I am free to be a voluntary servant to others.

PRAYER: Lord, I acknowledge that I am your slave. Thank you for the freedom to live a life that is pleasing to you. Amen.

Part III

Shem

10

Is everyone a descendant of Noah?

And how is it that we each hear them in our own language to which we were born? Parthians and Medes and Elamites, and residents of Mesopotamia, Judea and Cappadocia, Pontus and Asia, Phrygia and Pamphylia, Egypt and the districts of Libya around Cyrene, and visitors from Rome, both Jews and proselytes, Cretans and Arabs—we hear them in our own tongues speaking of the mighty deeds of God.

Acts 2:8–11 (NASB)

Human history is riddled with ethnic conflicts. Recent decades have seen Israeli versus Arab in Palestine, Serb versus Albanian in Kosovo, Arab versus Persian in Iraq, Hutu versus Tutsi in Rwanda, and black versus white in America. Such conflicts express hatred of one ethnic group toward another bolstered by grievances accumulated over centuries. What does the Bible say about ethnic groups?

Genesis 10:1–32 (NASB)

III. SHEM

A. GENEALOGY OF SHEM, HAM, AND JAPHETH

1. Title

CHAPTER 10

1 Now these are the **genealogies** of the generations of Shem, Ham, and Japheth, the sons of Noah; and **descendants** were born to them after the flood.

2. Sons of Japheth

2 The **descendants** of Japheth were Gomer and Magog and Madai and Javan and Tubal and Meshech and Tiras.

3 The **descendants** of Gomer were Ashkenaz and Riphath and Togarmah.

4 The **descendants** of Javan were Elishah and Tarshish, Kittim and Dodanim.

5 From these the coastlands of the nations were separated into their lands, every one according to his language, according to their families, into their nations.

3. Sons of Ham

6 The **descendants** of Ham were Cush and Mizraim and Put and Canaan.

7 The **descendants** of Cush were Seba and Havilah and Sabtah and Raamah and Sabteca; and the **descendants** of Raamah were Sheba and Dedan.

8 Now Cush became the **ancestor** of Nimrod; he became a mighty one on the **land**. 9 He was a mighty hunter before the Lord; therefore it is said, "Like Nimrod a mighty hunter before the Lord." 10 The beginning of his kingdom was Babel and Erech and Accad and Calneh, in the land of Shinar. 11 From that land he went forth into Assyria, and built Nineveh and Rehoboth-Ir and Calah, 12 and Resen between Nineveh and Calah; that is the great city.

13 Mizraim became the **ancestor** of Ludim and Anamim and Lehabim and Naphtuhim 14 and Pathrusim and Casluhim (from which came the Philistines) and Caphtorim.

15 Canaan became the **ancestor** of Sidon, his firstborn, and Heth 16 and the Jebusite and the Amorite and the Girgashite 17 and the Hivite and the Arkite and the Sinite 18 and the Arvadite and the Zemarite and the Hamathite; and afterward the families of the Canaanite were spread abroad.

19 The territory of the Canaanite extended from Sidon as you go toward Gerar, as far as Gaza; as you go toward Sodom and Gomorrah and Admah and Zeboiim, as far as Lasha.

20 These are the **descendants** of Ham, according to their families, according to their languages, by their lands, by their nations.

4. Sons of Shem

21 Also to Shem, the **ancestor** of all the children of Eber, and the older brother of Japheth, children were born. 22 The **descendants** of Shem were Elam and Asshur and Arpachshad and Lud and Aram.

23 The **descendants** of Aram were Uz and Hul and Gether and Mash.

24 Arpachshad became the **ancestor** of Shelah; and Shelah became the **ancestor** of Eber.

25 Two sons were born to Eber; the name of the one was Peleg, for in his days the **land** was divided; and his brother's name was Joktan.

26 Joktan became the **ancestor** of Almodad and Sheleph and Hazarmaveth and Jerah 27 and Hadoram and Uzal and Diklah 28 and Obal and Abimael and Sheba 29 and Ophir and Havilah and Jobab; all these were the **descendants** of Joktan.

30 Now their settlement extended from Mesha as you go toward Sephar, the hill country of the east.

31 These are the **descendants** of Shem, according to their families, according to their languages, by their lands, according to their nations.

5. Epilogue

32 These are the families of the sons of Noah, according to their genealogies, by their nations; and out of these the nations were separated on the **land** after the flood.

Genesis 10:1 and 10:32 frame this genealogy by using similar phrases. Seven sons and seven grandsons[1] indicate whole families. A narrative epilogue marks the end of the section.

Mizraim (NASB)[2] is often translated *Egypt*. The ending *-im* in Hebrew frequently indicates plural, such as members of a nation.[3]

Is everyone a descendant of Noah?

The traditional interpretation says the descendants of Noah listed in this passage are representative of all the world's ethic groups. Secular anthropologists propose complex theories of migration and cultural interaction to explain the origin of ethnic groups. Is everyone a descendant of Noah?

The key to answering this question is "Was the Flood global or local?" Obviously, if the Flood covered Planet Earth, then Noah's family members were the only survivors, and so everyone since then is his descendant. An earlier chapter discussed this issue. My opinion is that the Flood was a local catastrophe.

There are seventy names in the genealogy of Shem, Ham, and Japheth. (Philistines are not counted in the seventy; similarly, Nimrod's kingdom[4] and the cities of Canaan[5] are not counted.) Because seventy (seven times ten) is associated with wholeness and many translations say *earth*, many interpret this

---

[1]For example, 10:2–4.
[2]10:6. The Hebrew word *mizraim* (*Strong's* No. 4714).
[3]Such as in 10:13–14 (NASB).
[4]10:10–12.
[5]10:19.

genealogy as global in scope. Throughout this book, I translate the Hebrew as **land** rather than *earth*[6] to emphasize that Planet Earth was not intended.

The names correspond to many of the nationalities known at the time Genesis was written. These seventy names became labels for people-groups. "Families" (NASB), "nations," and "languages" are three ways to categorize people.[7] *Families* indicates relationships through blood or marriage. *Nations* does not indicate blood relatives, but rather common cultures (Speiser, 1967). *Languages* refers to those who learned common languages. Thus, everyone in an ethnic group was not necessarily a descendant of the group's famous namesake. Genesis 9:19 says the whole **land** was populated by Noah's family, but Genesis does not claim that these are the only nations, nor does this genealogy claim that everyone on Planet Earth is a descendant of Noah. Moreover, the Bible does not try to explain complex patterns of migration and cultural interaction. The Bible does not tell me where all the ethnic groups of Planet Earth came from, but Genesis does indicate that Noah's descendants spread out after the Flood.

Are ethnic groups important to God?

The migration and cultural interactions of ethnic groups may be interesting, but it is more important to me to know what God thinks about ethnic groups. Rather than focus on the history of ancient nations, let us ask, "Are ethnic groups important to God?"

Because seventy is associated with wholeness, these nations can be interpreted as representing the totality of humanity. Even though the passage is not global in a historical sense, the Bible teaches that all of mankind across Planet Earth is one family from God's perspective.[8] The nations in this genealogy all have a common relationship to Noah and his sons, but each one also has its own identity.

The Old Testament focuses on the descendants of Abraham—the nation of Israel, the Jewish people. God chose to have a special relationship with that ethnic group. However, the Council of Jerusalem (about AD 49) did not require gentile Christians to become Jews.[9] The New Testament gospel does not ask people to give up their ethnic identity to join some specially favored group. I am free to keep my ethnic identity. The gospel reaches across ethnic boundaries, because God loves the whole world.[10] God loves me irrespective of my ethnic identity.

People from other cultures may seem strange to me. They may have their own clothing styles, foods, languages, holidays, histories, religions, and values. They are different from me. If I am going to love my international neigh-

---

[6]The Hebrew word *'eres* (*Strong's* No. 776).

[7]10:5, 20, 31, 32.

[8]Ephesians 3:14–15.

[9]Acts 15:1–29.

[10]John 3:16.

bors, as God commanded, then I must make an effort to learn about their cultures as I get to know them. Understanding their cultures will equip me to love them better.

> There is no distinction between Greek and Jew, circumcised and uncircumcised, barbarian, Scythian, slave and freeman, but Christ is all, and in all.
>
> Colossians 3:11 (NASB)

How do you pronounce your name?

Read Genesis 10:1–32.

There is no Jew or Greek, slave or free, male or female; for you are all one in Christ Jesus.

Galatians 3:28 (HCSB)

A Chinese student came to my office for some academic help. When I said her name, she replied that I was the first person in America to pronounce her name correctly. My efforts to learn Chinese names had paid off.

I encounter people from various ethnic backgrounds all the time. Names are often difficult to pronounce. If I will make a concerted effort to learn to pronounce names correctly, their faces light up, because it shows that I care about them as individuals. God loves people from all nations.

PRAYER: Lord, help me to love people from around the world the way you do. Help me reach across barriers of language and culture with your love. Amen.

11

Why are there many languages?

> After this I looked, and there before me was a great multitude that no one could count, from every ...language, standing before the throne and before the Lamb. They were wearing white robes and were holding palm branches in their hands.
>
> Revelation 7:9 (NIV)

I had a summer job in Germany, but I had studied German for only one year in high school. I could say, "How is the weather today?" but not much else. I was thankful for a few German friends and coworkers who spoke English, but mostly I felt isolated, missing out on the conversations around me. I found studying a foreign language very difficult and hard work. There are many languages today around the world that isolate visitors from the local folks.

What does the Bible say about the origin of languages?

Genesis 11:1–9 (NASB)

B. TOWER OF BABEL

1. Sin of Pride

CHAPTER 11

1 Now the whole **land** used the same language and the same words. 2 It came about as they journeyed east, that they found a plain in the land of Shinar and settled there.

3 They said to one another, "Come, let us make bricks and burn them thoroughly." And they used brick for stone, and they used tar for mortar. 4 They said, "Come, let us build for ourselves a city,

and a tower whose top will reach into **the sky**, and let us make for
ourselves a name, otherwise we will be scattered abroad over the
face of the whole **land**."

      2. Judgment

  5 The Lord came down to see the city and the tower which the
sons of **mankind** had built. 6 The Lord said, "Behold, they are one
people, and they all have the same language. And this is what they
began to do, and now nothing which they purpose to do will be impossible for them. 7 Come, let Us go down and there confuse their
language, so that they will not understand one another's speech."

  8 So the Lord scattered them abroad from there over the face of
the whole **land**; and they stopped building the city.

    9 Therefore its name was called Babel, because there the
    Lord confused the language of the whole **land**;

and from there the Lord scattered them abroad over the face of the
whole **land**.

  The outline of the story of the Tower of Babel consists of sin and its judgment. The end of the story is marked by a naming and a narrative epilogue.[1]

  This story has many wordplays and alliterations in Hebrew (Sailhamer,
2008, pp. 144–145) which emphasize the key role of language in the story. *Make
for ourselves a name* (NASB)[2] is wordplay on *Shem* which means *name* (Sailhamer, 2008, p. 143). Shem's genealogy is in the previous passage. *Babel*[3] is usually
translated *Babylon*. However, wordplay is intended here like English *babble*, so
English translations traditionally use *Babel* here instead of *Babylon*.

Why are there many languages?

The languages of Planet Earth have an amazing variety of sounds and patterns. To the untrained ear, a foreign language sounds like gibberish, but each
language conveys meaning to those who know it. Why are there many languages?

  The story of the Tower of Babel says the Lord confused the builders of a
temple-tower through language. As a result of the confusion, they quit building the tower and went to various places. The traditional interpretation attributes the origin of Planet Earth's languages to this incident. Linguists propose complex theories of gradual differentiation and assimilation of languages.
They say languages gradually have changed and influenced each other ever
since prehistoric times. This mismatch is confusing.

---

[1]11:9.
[2]11:4.
[3]The Hebrew word *babel* (*Strong's* No. 894).

Like other passages, traditional translations make it seem that the story is about Planet Earth. *The whole earth* (NASB)[4] is better translated *the whole* **land**, because it refers to a particular geographic location, the region of Babylon. Genesis 10:10 indicates that Nimrod's kingdom included Babylon (Babel). As discussed in an earlier chapter, I think the Flood was a local catastrophe, so I don't think the entire population of Planet Earth was in Babylon at this time.

The passage does not say how the Lord confused their language, nor how many distinct languages resulted from this incident. The passage does not claim to explain the origin of Planet Earth's languages.

Is civilization good?

Rather than an explanation of languages, the story of the Tower of Babel gives insight into civilizations. Many assume that civilization is a good thing, because mankind has achieved unprecedented prosperity, conquered diseases, extended life spans, reduced infant mortality, and so on. On the other hand, civilizations are also the source of wars and oppression. Is civilization good?

The people of Babylon desired to reach the sky. This indicates they were challenging God's authority. They wanted to be famous as a path to a kind of immortality. They also were disobeying the mandate given to Noah's sons to populate the land.[5] The story establishes Babylon as the archetype of worldly civilization—arrogant, ambitious, and rebellious toward the Lord.

Archeology has confirmed that temple-towers were built in Babylon from its earliest times. Such temple-towers are examples of the monumental public works that have characterized civilizations throughout history. History text-books often point to such architecture with pride.

Wells (1989) explains that Western civilization reflects many non-Christian influences, from ancient Greece and Rome to atheist philosophies of the Enlightenment. Civilizations in general, and our own culture in particular, celebrate the pride of mankind, and are antagonistic to the ways of the Lord.

The Lord limited what they could achieve in Babylon. The Tower of Babel was a local event that reminds us that civilization is not fundamentally good. When worldly civilizations are evaluated in light of biblical principles, we see evidence that "all have sinned and fall short of the glory of God."[6] Worldly civilization, pictured as Babylon in Revelation 17 and 18 will fall when Jesus returns,[7] and he will reign over Planet Earth with righteousness.

> And another angel, a second one, followed, saying, "Fallen, fallen is Babylon the great, she who has made all the nations drink of the wine of the passion of her immorality."
>
> Revelation 14:8 (NASB)

---

[4]11:1.
[5]9:7.
[6]Romans 3:23 (NASB).
[7]Revelation 17:1–18:24.

My civilization

Read Genesis 11:4.

Why are the nations in an uproar
And the peoples devising a vain thing?
The kings of the earth take their stand
And the rulers take counsel together
Against the Lord and against His Anointed.

Psalms 2:1–2 (NASB)

The United Nations Security Council is meeting over another crisis. Refugees are streaming from the region to avoid the fighting. Famine is imminent. Winter is coming. Angry speeches go back and forth. Frantic negotiations go on behind closed doors. Another hot spot needs peacekeepers.

Even though I grew up in Western Civilization, I am a citizen of the kingdom of heaven. Jesus is its king and the Bible reveals how citizens like me should live. I am determined to live a kingdom lifestyle even though I am surrounded by corrupt Western Civilization. When Jesus reigns on Planet Earth, corruption will be replaced by righteousness. I can imagine how world leaders will react when he returns.

PRAYER: Lord, the kingdom of heaven is my civilization. Help me to live your lifestyle faithfully until you come again. Amen.

12

When was the Flood?

When He began His ministry, Jesus Himself was about thirty years of age, being, as was supposed, the son of Joseph, the son of Eli, ... the son of Shem ... the son of Enosh, the son of Seth, the son of Adam, the son of God.

Luke 3:23–38 (NASB)

I was preparing a family tree. I realized that a new branch was needed, because John Henry, my first cousin twice removed, was born the other day. Keeping track of the family can be complicated. The names, dates, places, and events help me trace the history of the family and who is related to whom today.

What does the Bible say about Shem's family?

Genesis 11:10–26 (NASB)

C. GENEALOGY OF SHEM

1. Title

10 These are the **genealogies** of the generations of Shem.

2. Sons

Shem was one hundred years old, and became the **ancestor** of Arpachshad two years after the flood; 11 and Shem lived five hundred years after he became the **ancestor** of Arpachshad, and he had other sons and daughters.

12 Arpachshad lived thirty-five years, and became the **ancestor** of Shelah; 13 and Arpachshad lived four hundred and three years after he became the **ancestor** of Shelah, and he had other sons and daughters.

14 Shelah lived thirty years, and became the **ancestor** of Eber; 15 and Shelah lived four hundred and three years after he became the **ancestor** of Eber, and he had other sons and daughters.

16 Eber lived thirty-four years, and became the **ancestor** of Peleg; 17 and Eber lived four hundred and thirty years after he became the **ancestor** of Peleg, and he had other sons and daughters.

18 Peleg lived thirty years and became the **ancestor** of Reu; 19 and Peleg lived two hundred and nine years after he became the **ancestor** of Reu, and he had other sons and daughters.

20 Reu lived thirty-two years, and became the **ancestor** of Serug; 21 and Reu lived two hundred and seven years after he became the **ancestor** of Serug, and he had other sons and daughters.

22 Serug lived thirty years, and became the **ancestor** of Nahor; 23 and Serug lived two hundred years after he became the **ancestor** of Nahor, and he had other sons and daughters.

24 Nahor lived twenty-nine years, and became the **ancestor** of Terah; 25 and Nahor lived one hundred and nineteen years after he became the **ancestor** of Terah, and he had other sons and daughters.

26 Terah lived seventy years, and became the father of Abram, Nahor and Haran.

This genealogy consists simply of a title and short paragraphs about each patriarch. The paragraph on Terah is completed later.[1]

The genealogy of Shem lacks a marker denoting the end (such as poetry plus narrative), but it does introduce Abraham, the next patriarch.[2] Therefore in my outline, I put this genealogy at the end of the section on Shem. The genealogy of Shem has ten names from Shem to Abraham, a round number in ancient Mesopotamia and Egypt.

When was the Flood?

Bishop James Ussher (1581–1656) is famous for his calendar that dated the creation of the universe as 4004 BC. Modern archeology has found many sites that are much older. Was Bishop Ussher mistaken? A key point of reference in his calculation was the date of the Flood. When was Noah's Flood?

The genealogy of Shem is the traditional basis for calculating the year of Noah's Flood. Based on other Scriptures, modern scholars estimate that Abraham was born about 2166 BC (Barker, 1995, *s.v.* timeline chart). A traditional interpretation of Shem's genealogy calculates that the Flood was in 2458 BC.

As we have noted in earlier chapters, a genealogy names ancestors, rather than direct father-son relationships. So the lives of these patriarchs did not necessarily overlap. If one translates *father* (NASB) to mean **ancestor**, then the Flood was some time before the traditional date.

Other Genesis stories give us some clues that bracket when the Flood could have occurred, but do not imply a date. For example, in the story of Cain

---

[1] 11:32.
[2] Abram was given the name *Abraham* later.

and Abel, *flocks* implies domesticated animal husbandry, and *tiller of the ground* (NASB) implies domesticated plants—agriculture.[3] Archeology has found evidence of agriculture about 10 000 BC (Fischer, 1993). So the Flood probably happened after agriculture was discovered. Tubal-Cain[4] practiced metallurgy. He was the sixth patriarch after Cain. However, Genesis does not tell us which of Cain's descendants were contemporaries of which of Seth's descendants. Yamauchi (1993) explains the development of metallurgy in the ancient world. Copper artifacts from about 6000 BC have been discovered. Before metallurgy, people made cutting tools from flint and other rocks.

Because the genealogy is not necessarily direct father-son relationships, we cannot calculate the years from Noah to Abraham.

Was the Messiah human?

Over the centuries, some have claimed that Jesus, the Messiah, was not actually human, but rather, was only a divine spirit in human form. From the earliest times, the church fathers have rejected this doctrine as a heresy. If the Messiah was human, then he had to have ancestors. The genealogies of Genesis answer the question, "Who were the ancestors of the Messiah?" The "Who?" question is important, because it answers the question, "Was the Messiah human?"

God promised the Messiah would be an Israelite. Abraham was the father of the Israelites. The Genealogy of Mankind,[5] the Genealogy of Noah,[6] and the Genealogy of Shem[7] link Abraham back to Adam, who was certainly human.

In chapter 11, Shem's genealogy is traced through Peleg[8] rather than his brother Joktan.[9] The promise of redemption is traced through a line of godly ancestors, namely, Adam,[10] Enoch,[11] Noah,[12] Abraham,[13] and others. God was faithful, and from time to time, established covenants with some. Each covenant was a local event with significance for us. The genealogy of Shem[14] is a link in the chain from the promise given to Eve[15] to the birth of the Messiah.[16] God had it planned from the beginning. Yes, the Messiah had ancestors and was human. Because he was a human being, he could die for mankind's sin. His death paid the penalty for my sin.

---

[3] 4:2.
[4] 4:22.
[5] 5:1–6:4.
[6] 6:9–10.
[7] 11:10–26.
[8] 11:18.
[9] 10:21–31.
[10] 2:15.
[11] 5:24.
[12] 6:9.
[13] 12:1–4.
[14] 11:10–26.
[15] 3:15.
[16] Luke 3:23–38.

Genealogy

Read Genesis 11:10–26.

These all died in faith without having received the promises, but they saw them from a distance, greeted them, and confessed that they were foreigners and temporary residents on the earth.

Hebrews 11:13 (HCSB)

Family genealogy is a hobby for several of my relatives. They have identified some ancestors born in England in the 1600s. Others were from Germany in the 1700s and 1800s. Sometimes there is an interesting story, and sometimes just a name. Jacob Freese (1788–1873) permitted no work on Sundays. Amos Williams Davis (1829–1906) taught Bible classes for many years, and always sat near the pulpit in the "Amen corner." My best photo of Ethel Baughman (1887–1971) shows her reading her Bible.

I am thankful for the positive influence of godly ancestors on later generations, even down to me.

PRAYER: Lord, help me to be a good example to the younger generation like the ancestors who came before me. Amen.

Part IV

Abraham

13

Does God talk to ordinary people?

> [God said], "I will surely bless you and I will surely multiply you."
> And so, having patiently waited, [Abraham] obtained the promise.
>
> Hebrews 6:14–15 (NASB)

When good friends get together, they can talk and talk and talk. Perhaps over a meal or while taking a walk, the conversation rolls on and on. Can anyone be God's friend? Moses talked with God as a friend. Adam, Enoch, and Noah walked with God. Jesus talked with his heavenly Father and said we can, too. I want to know God like a friend. What does the Bible say about Abraham's friendship with God?

Genesis 11:27–12:4 (NIV)

IV. ABRAHAM

A. GENEALOGY OF TERAH

1. Title

27 Now these are the **genealogies** of the generations of Terah.

2. Sons

Terah became the father of Abram, Nahor and Haran.

And Haran became the father of Lot. 28 Haran died in the presence of his father Terah in the land of his birth, in Ur of the Chaldeans.

29 Abram and Nahor took wives for themselves. The name of Abram's wife was Sarai; and the name of Nahor's wife was Milcah,

the daughter of Haran, the father of Milcah and Iscah. 30 Sarai was barren; she had no child.

31 Terah took Abram his son, and Lot the son of Haran, his grandson, and Sarai his daughter-in-law, his son Abram's wife; and they went out together from Ur of the Chaldeans in order to enter the land of Canaan; and they went as far as Haran, and settled there.

B. GENEALOGY OF SHEM COMPLETED

32 The days of Terah were two hundred and five years; and Terah died in Haran.

C. PROMISE

CHAPTER 12

1 Now the Lord said to Abram,

> "Go forth from your country,
> And from your relatives
> And from your father's house,
> To the land which I will show you;
> 2 And I will make you a great nation,
> And I will bless you,
> And make your name great;
> And so you shall be a blessing;
> 3 And I will bless those who bless you,
> And the one who curses you I will curse.
> And in you all the families of the earth will be blessed."

4 So Abram went forth as the Lord had spoken to him; and Lot went with him. Now Abram was seventy-five years old when he departed from Haran...

(The story of Abraham continues)

The genealogy of Terah is delimited by a title at the beginning[1] and a narrative epilogue at the end[2] similar to the earlier genealogies. The statement about Terah's death[3] completes the pattern of the Genealogy of Shem.[4]

Abram was later given the name *Abraham*,[5] which is more familiar to modern readers. Similarly, Sarai was later given the name *Sarah*.[6] This passage clearly teaches that Terah was the father of Abraham,[7] rather than a distant an-

---

[1] 11:27.
[2] 11:32.
[3] 11:32.
[4] 11:26.
[5] 17:5.
[6] 17:15.
[7] 11:31.

cestor. The story places Abraham's family in Mesopotamia in the city of Ur.[8] Details of Terah's genealogy here give background that is important later in the story of Abraham, but beyond the limits of this book.

Does God talk to ordinary people?

When we read biblical stories, it seems that God spoke to spiritual giants long ago and far away, such as Adam and Noah. Does God talk to ordinary people, too?

In this passage, Abraham seems like a pretty ordinary guy. Genesis 12:1 says that God spoke to him. While the family lived in Ur, the Lord told Abraham to go to a land that the Lord would show him.[9] Terah began to move the family to the land of Canaan,[10] but settled along the way in northern Mesopotamia.[11] After Terah died Abraham completed the journey.[12] These verses are just the beginning of Abraham's journey of faith.[13] Genesis 12 opens with God's promise to Abraham and his response. In faith, Abraham followed the direction of the Lord. Abraham did not know where the Lord would lead him, nor what it would be like when he got there, but he obeyed anyway.

The obedience of Abraham is an example to me. The story of Abraham shows that God honors a person's heart attitude. Abraham did not gain God's favor by following correct religious procedures. Faith in the Lord was what counted for Abraham, and it is the only thing that counts today.[14] Yes, God speaks to ordinary people, and ordinary people can respond in faith, just like Abraham did.

> For what does the Scripture say? "Abraham believed God, and it was credited to him as righteousness."
>
> Romans 4:3 (NASB)

---

[8]Ur was in southern modern Iraq.
[9]Acts 7:2–3.
[10]The land of Canaan was modern Palestine.
[11]11:31.
[12]12:4 and Acts 7:4.
[13]Hebrews 11:8–19.
[14]15:6.

An ordinary person

Read Genesis 12:1.

[May God] equip you with all that is good to do His will,
working in us what is pleasing in His sight, through Jesus
Christ.

Hebrews 13:21 (HCSB)

I was considering whether to quit my job and go back to school. This
was a big decision. I needed guidance from the Lord. As I read about
Abraham, the words seemed to jump off the page. I heard the Lord
speak softly, not audibly, to my soul. The Holy Spirit told me that in
teaching, I would affect many lives. This was very encouraging.

Later, I was doubting whether I could succeed in school. As I read
the book of Hebrews, again the words seemed to jump off the page. The
Lord reassured me that he would equip me to succeed in the journey
toward a teaching career.

I am not anyone special. God talks to ordinary people, like me.

PRAYER: Lord, thank you for talking to me through Holy
Spirit and the Bible. Amen.

14

Final remarks

A gentle answer turns away wrath,
But a harsh word stirs up anger.

Proverbs 15:1 (NASB)

Christians and atheists often debate whether Genesis 1 through 11 is true. The Christian wants to show that God exists and uses the Bible for support. The atheist wants to show that the Bible is not true, and so he attacks the stories in Genesis as unscientific. The debate goes back and forth, becoming more and more heated. Anger takes over from discussion. The rest of us are just confused. I'm just looking for honest answers to honest questions.

My faith is in God, and I'm confident the Bible, the Word of God, is true. However, I was unsatisfied both with the traditional literal reading of Genesis and with the atheists' science-based challenges. So I embarked on this study of Genesis 1 through 11.

Each chapter title of this book is a controversial question where tradition gives a pat answer, but an atheist would say the Bible is just fanciful myths. To many of these questions, I have concluded that the Bible does not give an answer. So, atheists' attacks are irrelevant to the Bible, and debate becomes unnecessary. To other questions, a close look at the passage yields clear answers. Each chapter of this book also considers deeper questions that are answered by Genesis. After all is said, the Word of God is still true. The sections below follow the outline of Genesis 1 through 11, summarizing the discussion of questions considered.

I. Adam

A. Creation of the Sky and Land (1:1–2:3)

How long did Creation take? The traditional answer is six days. However, Genesis is not a newspaper with a complete chronology of facts. I think the

Bible does not say how long Creation took, because the word *day* can be interpreted as an indefinite era, rather than a twenty-four hour day.

Who created the universe? God did. The "Who?" question is more important to me than the "How long?" question. All the universe was made by God's power at his initiative for his purposes.

Did evolution really happen? The traditional answer is "No." Six twenty-four hour days is too short a time for evolution, and the order of events in Genesis 1 does not match evolutionary theory. The multifaceted literary structure of Genesis 1 is evidence that it does not present events in chronological order. I conclude that the Bible does not deny that all the variety of life was the result of biological evolution. Genesis is not a science lesson.

Why did God create life? God wanted to bless his creatures and mankind. The Creator of the universe prepared a good place for mankind to live.

> Seeing that His divine power has granted to us everything pertaining to life and godliness, through the true knowledge of Him who called us by His own glory and excellence.
>
> 2 Peter 1:3 (NASB)

B. Genealogy of the Sky and the Land (2:4–24)

Did mankind come from monkeys? The traditional answer is mankind was a special creation of God. Mainstream science claims monkeys and mankind have a common ancestor. I think the images of a potter for males and a surgeon for females are figurative ways to say that mankind's body is the same stuff as dirt and that male and female bodies are similar stuff. So, I think the Bible does not address the process the Lord God used to create the body of anatomically modern man. But the Bible does teach that the origin of mankind was in the heart of the Lord God.

What is mankind's purpose? Mankind's purpose is to worship and obey the Lord. The man's purpose in the Garden of Eden was to fellowship with the Lord God. When I do this, I am fulfilling my highest purpose in life.

> The conclusion, when all has been heard, is: fear God and keep His commandments, because this applies to every person.
>
> Ecclesiastes 12:13 (NASB)

C. Fall (2:25–3:24)

Are people naturally good? No, everyone sins like Adam and Eve did. However, Jesus died so that we can receive righteousness through him.

Who is responsible for sin?   Everyone is accountable for his own actions, just like Adam and Eve were each responsible for theirs. Like them, I have experienced forgiveness that covers my sin and embarrassment. The doctrine of Original Sin is a important theological concept that deserves more discussion, because the question "How did sin enter the world?" is too similar to the pagan story of Pandora's Box.

> The person who sins will die. The son will not bear the punishment for the father's iniquity, nor will the father bear the punishment for the son's iniquity; the righteousness of the righteous will be upon himself, and the wickedness of the wicked will be upon himself. … "For I have no pleasure in the death of anyone who dies," declares the Lord God. "Therefore, repent and live."
>
> Ezekiel 18:20,32 (NASB)

D. Cain and Abel (4:1–26)

Is revenge acceptable?   No, only God has the right to vengeance. Cain expected to be killed by an avenger, but the mercy of God gave Cain protection from human vengeance.

What style of worship is best?   The types of offerings of Cain and Abel were not important. Offerings made in faith are better than religious ritual, so style is not very important to God.

> Samuel said [to Saul],
>
> "Has the Lord as much delight in burnt offerings and sacrifices
> As in obeying the voice of the Lord?
> Behold, to obey is better than sacrifice,
> And to heed than the fat of rams.
> For rebellion is as the sin of divination,
> And insubordination is as iniquity and idolatry.
> Because you have rejected the word of the Lord,
> He has also rejected you from being king."
>
> 1 Samuel 15:22–23 (NASB)

E. Genealogy of Mankind (5:1–6:4)

How long did the patriarchs live?   According to a traditional literal interpretation, the patriarchs had surprisingly long lives without any indication of why they were different from lifespans today. The appendix presents some speculation on how the large numbers could have been a symbolic way to give them honor. I don't have a good answer for why the patriarchs' lifespans are large numbers.

Who was mankind's father?   Genesis 5 does not say who, if anyone, preceded Adam, but it does say the Lord God was the ultimate source of mankind. Jesus said I have a heavenly Father with whom I can talk whenever I want.

> He who has My commandments and keeps them is the one who loves Me; and he who loves Me will be loved by My Father, and I will love him and will disclose Myself to him.
>
> John 14:21 (NASB)

II. Noah

A. Corruption of the Land (6:5–8)

B. Genealogy of Noah (6:9–10)

C. Flood of the Land (6:11–9:17)

Did the Flood cover all of Planet Earth?   The traditional answer is "Yes." The Bible teaches that Noah's Flood was an historical event, not just a myth. The Hebrew word often translated *earth* is better translated **land**, and so, does not imply Planet Earth. In my opinion, the account in Genesis is consistent with a local catastrophe that destroyed all the inhabited land known to Noah.

Does God keep his promises?   God was faithful to Noah, who walked with him. The sign of the rainbow is God's guarantee that the next judgment will not be a flood; the Bible tells us it will be by fire. God kept his promise of a savior through the seed of Eve, and he has promised me eternal life. Yes, God keeps his promises.

> The Lord is faithful to all his promises
> and loving toward all he has made.
>
> Psalms 145:13b (NIV)

D. Noah's Curse (9:18–27)

Does Noah's curse justify racial prejudice?   Of course not. Noah's cursing of Canaan is not valid justification for the tragic enslaving of Africans by Europeans, and does not justify racist attitudes today.

How can one honor others?   Shem and Japheth honored their father by covering his embarrassment. Love for others forgives offenses and refuses gossip.

> Above all, keep fervent in your love for one another, because love covers a multitude of sins.
>
> 1 Peter 4:8 (NASB)

E. Genealogy of Mankind Completed (9:28-29)

III. Shem

A. Genealogy of Shem, Ham, and Japheth (10:1–32)

Is everyone a descendant of Noah?   Because the traditional interpretation assumes that the Flood covered Planet Earth, it follows that everyone is a descendant of Noah. This passage says Noah was an ancestor to the namesakes of seventy nations. Because a local Flood allows others to have survived in places unknown to Noah, I don't think Genesis implies all the ethnic groups on Planet Earth descended from Noah.

Are ethnic groups important to God?   I don't have to give up my ethnic identity to follow Jesus, but it's not very important. All of mankind is one family from God's perspective.

> For this reason I bow my knees before the Father, from whom every family in heaven and on earth derives its name,
>
> Ephesians 3:14–15 (NASB)

B. Tower of Babel (11:1–9)

Why are there many languages?   The traditional interpretation assumes the Tower of Babel story happened shortly after a global Flood, so this event is assumed to be the initial cause for Planet Earth's many languages. The Tower of Babel story may explain the origin of some languages, but I don't think Genesis explains the origin of languages on Planet Earth in general, because the Tower of Babel story was a local event.

Is civilization good?   No, civilization is not fundamentally good. The story of the Tower of Babel is an example of how civilizations rebel against the Lord. But God is still in charge, and he will have the final say.

> And [the angel] cried out with a mighty voice, saying, "Fallen, fallen is Babylon the great! She has become a dwelling place of demons and a prison of every unclean spirit, and a prison of every unclean and hateful bird. For all the nations have drunk of the wine of the passion of her immorality, and the kings of the earth have committed acts of immorality with her, and the merchants of the earth have become rich by the wealth of her sensuality."
>
> Revelation 18:2–3 (NASB)

C. Genealogy of Shem (11:10–26)

When was the Flood?   The traditional reading considers genealogies to list direct father-son relationships. However, the Hebrew word translated *begat* (KJV) can mean *became the ancestor of.* So, genealogies in Genesis do not necessarily list all the direct father-son relationships between Noah and Abraham. Thus, I think one cannot calculate the date of the Flood from the genealogies in Genesis.

Was the Messiah human?   Yes, Jesus, the Messiah, had ancestors, and thus, was human. Genesis lists honored ancestors of Abraham, the founding father of the Israelites, and the Messiah was a descendant of Abraham.

> When He began His ministry, Jesus Himself was about thirty years of age, being, as was supposed, the son of Joseph, the son of Eli, ...the son of Jacob, the son of Isaac, the son of Abraham, the son of Terah, the son of Nahor, ...the son of Enosh, the son of Seth, the son of Adam, the son of God.
>
> Luke 3:23–38 (NASB)

IV. Abraham

A. Genealogy of Terah (11:27–31)

B. Genealogy of Shem Completed (11:32)

C. Promise (12:1–4)

Does God talk to ordinary people?   Yes, God spoke to Abraham when he was an ordinary person. Abraham responded in faith. Abraham's life is an example of faith in action for me to imitate.

> By faith Abraham, when he was called, obeyed by going out to a place which he was to receive for an inheritance; and he went out, not knowing where he was going. By faith he lived as an alien in the land of promise, as in a foreign land, dwelling in tents with Isaac and Jacob, fellow heirs of the same promise;
>
> Hebrews 11:8–9 (NASB)

Honest questions

> For the word of God is living and active and sharper than any two-edged sword, and piercing as far as the division of soul and spirit, of both joints and marrow, and able to judge the thoughts and intentions of the heart.
>
> Hebrews 4:12 (NASB)

God is not embarrassed by honest questions. He want me to understand his Word, the Bible, and he will help me as I study. I'm not interested in debating with an atheist. An atheist is only interested in discrediting the Bible. He relies on secular science for answers, especially the modern theory of evolution. The traditional Christian interpretation reads Genesis literally like a newspaper, assuming modern standards of journalism which were unknown when Genesis was written. Both are unsatisfying. I want to find the core message of Genesis and how it applies to my life, even if some questions remain unanswered.

In this study, I found Genesis presents local stories about real people that have significance for me, even though they are not written like a newspaper. They reveal how mankind sins, how God judges sin, and how God grants mercy and restoration.

> All Scripture is inspired by God and profitable for teaching, for reproof, for correction, for training in righteousness; so that the man of God may be adequate, equipped for every good work.
>
> 2 Timothy 3:16–17 (NASB)

APPENDIX

Speculation about Special Numbers

Numbers in Genesis are difficult to interpret (Sailhamer, 2008, pp. 111–112). Hill (2003) points out that certain numbers, such as 3, 7, 10, 40, 60, and 70, and numbers based on combinations, occur in the early chapters of Genesis much more frequently than other numbers. If numbers were only factual information, one would expect various numbers to be equally likely. This is not the case, so we need to look beyond the bare numbers.

The ancient pagan religions of Egypt and Mesopotamia used numbers for astrology and divination. Although scholars do not agree on the details of ancient numerology, ancient readers expected numbers to have symbolic meaning. The following lists some familiar numbers, associations with life in ancient times, and literary significance (C. A. Hill, 2003). Weaving these familiar numbers into the story with literary skill communicated qualities that bare facts cannot convey.

- 3 Seasons in Egypt—Complete

- 4 Directions (NSEW)—All the land

- 5 Digits on one hand

- 7 Days per week—Complete

- 10 Base of number system—Honor (Egypt and Mesopotamia)

- 12 Months per year—Complete

- 60 Base of number system—Honor (Mesopotamia)

- 100 Ten times ten—Great honor

Richards (1998, p. 77) explains that Egyptian numbers, at the time of Moses, were represented in base ten, similar to our number system. Numerals represented ones, tens, hundreds, etc. according to position. However, in Mesopotamia from before the time of Abraham, large numbers were represented in base sixty, so that some numerals represented sixties and powers of sixty. Numbers less than sixty were represented in base ten. Thus, ten and sixty were important round numbers in the cultures of that region. Moreover, Gillings (1972) explains that repeated doubling was a routine part of arithmetic in ancient Egypt. Thus, doubling a symbolic number emphasized its meaning.

The Old Testament condemns astrology and divination, so I do not think Moses intended a detailed mystical numerological interpretation. Moreover, I do not think that God encoded secret messages in the numbers for modern readers to discover, because the message of God's Word is for all of God's people in all eras, not just modern readers. Perhaps numbers in the early chapters of Genesis were intended to be broadly symbolic, and certain round numbers were associated with literary beauty or honor (C. A. Hill, 2003). This approach is not traditional and it is speculative.

Applying the above approach, Fischer (1994) and Hill (2003) propose non-literal interpretations of the long life spans of the patriarchs. Fischer (1994) proposes that, in the context of ancient Mesopotamian culture, the long life spans attributed to the patriarchs were intended to give them honor. Archeologists in Mesopotamia have found lists of ancient Sumerian kings which attribute life spans of thousands of years to the kings.

Hill (2003) also argues that the numbers in chapters 5 and 11 are symbolic, rather than literal, according to the ancient Mesopotamian world-view. The ages of the patriarchs revolve around the sacred numbers 60 and 7.[1] If the numbers are intended to honor the patriarchs symbolically, then we should look at the Hebrew phrasing, which the NASB closely follows. I imagine that as Genesis was read aloud to the ancient Israelites, the symbolic associations would have come to mind.

Some general patterns are evident in the genealogies of Genesis 5 and 11. Consider the patriarchs from Adam through Terah in reverse chronological order.[2] The following lists number phrases of the patriarchs' later years, when they "had other sons and daughters."

Patriarch. Years. Remark.

Terah. not stated: $205 - 70 = 35 + 100$. Most recent.
Nahor. 19 and 100. $19 = 7 + 12$ Sum of round numbers.
Serug. 200. Double the hundreds of Terah and Nahor.
Reu. 7 and 200.
Peleg. 9 and 200.
Eber. 30 and 400. Double the hundreds of Serug to Peleg.

---

[1]Hill (2003) also points out that five years is equivalent to 60 months.
[2]5:1–32, 9:28, and 11:10–26.

Shelah. 3 and 400.
Arphaxad. 3 and 400.
Shem. 500. Frame Noah.
Noah. 50 and 300. Years after the flood. Noah walked with God.
Lamech. 5 and 90 and 500. Frame Noah.
Methuselah. 2 and 80 and 700. $82 = 70 + 12$ Sum of round numbers.
    The oldest patriarch had a complete life.
Enoch. 300. Enoch walked with God.
Jared. 800. Double the hundreds of Eber to Arphaxad.
Mahalalel. 30 and 800.
Kenan. 40 and 800.
Enosh. 15 and 800.
Seth. 7 and 800.
Adam. 800. Most ancient.

Groups of patriarchs have 100, 200, 400, and 800 as part of the number phrase for their later years, progressing from recent patriarchs to ancient patriarchs. This may be significant, because Egyptian multiplication was based on multiplication by two (Gillings, 1972, p. 16). Perhaps Moses, who was educated in Egypt (or his sources), used multiplication by two to signify greater honor for more ancient patriarchs.

There are five exceptions out of these nineteen patriarchs. Methuselah's later years have seven hundreds, perhaps indicating a full complete life. Enoch's and Noah's later years each have three hundreds, perhaps giving them greater honor, because they each walked with God. Lamech, the father of Noah, and Shem, the son of Noah, have later years of five hundreds, framing the life of Noah.

The smaller numbers in each number phrase are ancient round numbers or the simple sum of round numbers. Perhaps these convey additional honor to the patriarchs.

A symbolic interpretation of the numbers is appealing, but I would like to know more about how people in ancient Mesopotamia viewed numbers like these. Perhaps archeology will find some evidence. One difficulty with Hill's approach is that the symbolic meaning of the numbers is not clear enough to explain why one differs from another. Another difficulty is this. Even if listeners in the time of Moses understood symbolic meanings, those meanings have been lost. If the meaning had been important to God's purpose, he would have found a way to communicate it from generation to generation. So maybe the lifespan question is not so important.

The bottom line is this approach is just speculation and the meaning of the lifespans of the patriarchs is not clear.

References

(2017). (Articles in *Perspectives on Science and Christian Faith* are available on-line at http://network.asa3.org/?page=PSCF (Current March 10, 2017). There is a delay from date of publication to availability online. Practically all articles are available online.)

Barker, K. (Ed.). (1995). *The NIV study Bible*. Grand Rapids, Michigan: Zonder-van.

Clarke, A. (1996). *Commentary* (Electronic Database ed.). Biblesoft. (Originally published 1817–1825.)

Clouser, R. (2016, December). Reading Genesis. *Perspectives on Science and Christian Faith, 68*(4), 237–261.

Cotterell, A. (1988). *China: A cultural history*. New York: Mentor Books.

Dake, F. J. (1963). *Dake's annotated reference Bible*. Lawrenceville, Georgia: Dake Bible Sales.

Fischer, D. (1993, December). In search of the historical Adam: Part I. *Perspectives on Science and Christian Faith, 45*(4), 241–251.

Fischer, D. (1994, March). In search of the historical Adam: Part II. *Perspectives on Science and Christian Faith, 46*(1), 47–57.

Gillings, R. J. (1972). *Mathematics in the times of the pharaohs*. Cambridge: MIT Press.

Goldenberg, D. M. (2005). *The curse of Ham: Race and slavery in early Judaism, Christianity, and Islam*. Princeton, New Jersey: Princeton University Press.

Haynes, S. R. (2002). *Noah's curse: The Biblical justification of American slavery*. Oxford: Oxford University Press.

Henry, M. (1991). *Commentary on the whole Bible* (New Modern Edition, Electronic Database ed.). Hendrickson Publishers.

Hill, A. E. (2006, June). Quantitative hydrology of Noah's flood. *Perspectives on Science and Christian Faith, 58*(2), 130–141.

Hill, C. A. (2000, March). The Garden of Eden: A modern landscape. *Perspectives on Science and Christian Faith, 52*(1), 31–46.

Hill, C. A. (2002, September). The Noachian flood: Universal or local? *Perspectives on Science and Christian Faith, 54*(3), 170–183.

Hill, C. A. (2003, December). Making sense of the numbers in Genesis. *Perspectives on Science and Christian Faith, 55*(4), 239–251.

Hill, C. A. (2006, June). Qualitative hydrology of Noah's flood. *Perspectives on Science and Christian Faith, 58*(2), 120–129.

Hurd, J. P. (2006, June). Reply to the real Adam and original sin. *Perspectives on Science and Christian Faith, 58*(2), 102–103.

Jeffers, J. S. (1999). *The Greco-Roman world of the New Testament era: Exploring the background of early Christianity*. Downers Grove, Illinois: InterVarsity Press.

Jet Propulsion Laboratory. (2013). *Planck mission brings universe into sharp focus*. NASA Press Release, March 21, 2013. (Available at http://www.jpl. nasa.gov/news/news.php?release=2013-109 (Current March 10, 2017))

Johnson, B. H. (1994, March). "In the beginning..." I think there was a big bang. *Perspectives on Science and Christian Faith, 45*(1), 58–60.

Kline, M. G. (1996, March). Space and time in the Genesis cosmogony. *Perspectives on Science and Christian Faith, 48*(1), 2–15.

Linder, D. O. (2000). *Scopes "Monkey" Trial (1925)* (Tech. Rep.). University of Missouri—Kansas City, School of Law. (Available at http://www. famous-trials.com/scopesmonkey (Current March 10, 2017).)

McIntyre, J. A. (2002, September). The historical Adam. *Perspectives on Science and Christian Faith, 54*(3), 150–157.

McIntyre, J. A. (2006a, June). The real Adam and original sin. *Perspectives on Science and Christian Faith, 58*(2), 90–98.

McIntyre, J. A. (2006b, June). A reply to the responders. *Perspectives on Science and Christian Faith, 58*(2), 106–108.

Murphy, G. L. (2006, June). Roads to paradise and perdition: Christ, evolution, and original sin. *Perspectives on Science and Christian Faith, 58*(2), 109–118.

Numbers, R. L. (1992). *The creationists: The evolution of scientific creationism*. Berkeley, California: University of California Press.

Phillips, P. G. (2005, June). The thrice-supported Big Bang. *Perspectives on Science and Christian Faith, 57*(2), 82–96.

Richards, E. G. (1998). *Mapping time: The calendar and its history*. Oxford: Oxford University Press.

Sailhamer, J. H. (1990). Genesis. In *The expositor's Bible commentary: Genesis–Numbers* (Vol. 2). Grand Rapids, Michigan: Zondervan.

Sailhamer, J. H. (2008). Genesis. In *The expositor's Bible commentary: Genesis–Leviticus* (Revised ed., Vol. 1). Grand Rapids, Michigan: Zondervan.

Seely, P. H. (2003, December). The GISP2 ice core: Ultimate proof that Noah's flood was not global. *Perspectives on Science and Christian Faith, 55*(4), 252–260.

Speiser, E. A. (1967). The rivers of Paradise. In J. J. Finkelstein & M. Greenberg (Eds.), *Oriental and Biblical studies: Collected writings of E. A. Speiser* (pp. 23–34). Philadelphia: University of Pennsylvania Press.

Spock, B. (1946). *The common sense book of baby and child care*. New York: Duell, Sloan, and Pearce.

Strong, J. (1894). *Exhaustive concordance of the Bible*. (Includes Hebrew and Greek dictionaries. This is a classic reference book. Its reference numbers for words are often used by other reference books.)

Tanner, W. F. (1996, March). Real world stratigraphy and the Noachian flood. *Perspectives on Science and Christian Faith, 48*(1), 44–47.

Tanner, W. F. (1997, June). 'Planet Earth'? or 'Land'? *Perspectives on Science and Christian Faith, 49*(2), 111–115.

Wells, R. A. (1989). *History through the eyes of faith: Western civilization and the kingdom of God.* New York: HarperCollins.

Whitcomb, J. C., & Morris, H. M. (1961). *The Genesis flood.* Institute for Creation Research.

Wilcox, D. (2006, June). The original Adam and the reality of sin. *Perspectives on Science and Christian Faith, 58*(2), 104–105.

Yamauchi, E. (1993, December). Metal sources and metallurgy in the Biblical world. *Perspectives on Science and Christian Faith, 45*(4), 252–259.

Yoder, P. (2006, June). Will the real Adam, please stand up! *Perspectives on Science and Christian Faith, 58*(2), 99–101.

Index

About the author

Edward B. Allen is the author of books for three styles of devotional Bible study. Verse-by-verse books draw devotional points from the Scripture passage in sequence. Historical-people books focus on incidents in the lives of historical people that illustrate biblical principles. Topical books explore relevant Scriptures throughout the Bible. His books also include many personal stories from modern life.

His books are in two series. Books in the *A Slow Walk* series have short meditations in daily-devotional format, such as *A Slow Walk through Psalm 119: 90 Devotional Meditations*. Books in the *Devotional Commentary* series are straight reads with a devotional slant, rather than academic or theological comments, such as *Practical Faith: A Devotional Commentary*.

He has led discussion Bible-study groups in evangelical churches for over 50 years He received a Ph.D. in Computer Science degree at Florida Atlantic University and had a career in software engineering. He has authored or coauthored over 80 professional papers.

www.ingramcontent.com/pod-product-compliance
Lightning Source LLC
Chambersburg PA
CBHW060312050426
42448CB00009B/1799